ON THE UP AND UP

ON THE UP AND UP

A SURVIVAL GUIDE FOR WOMEN LIVING WITH MEN ON THE DOWN LOW

Brenda Stone Browder
with Karen Hunter

KENSINGTON PUBLISHING CORP.

DAFINA BOOKS are published by

Kensington Publishing Corp.
850 Third Avenue
New York, NY 10022

ISBN 0-7582-1075-2

Printed in the United States of America

Contents

Foreword

FAITH UNDER FIRE

When I got the call to do the foreword for *On the Up and Up,* all I could say was, "Praise God!" Another woman has the courage to speak. There are many women, too many women, in relationships with men who they think they know but really don't. And there are too many women living lives that are lies and are too afraid to speak up and too afraid to do something about it.

Through a story like Brenda's and stories like mine and women like us who are willing to be honest and share, perhaps one less woman will go through what we endured. Perhaps one less woman has to die.

I learned that my husband had AIDS after a forty-five-day stay in the hospital for what I thought were complications from pneumonia. He had full-blown AIDS and was dying and I discovered that he knew he had the disease when he married me. Eleven months of dating and two years of marriage—it's funny that he never mentioned it.

He knew he had the disease, his mother knew he had the disease, his doctors knew, everyone seemed to know except me. And no one said a word.

I had no clue. At the end of his forty-five-day stay in the hospital he called a family conference where he made the announcement that he had the HIV virus. It was carefully orchestrated. I was devastated, but being the dutiful wife, I was going to stand by my man and be there for him. I was going to nurse him back to good health.

I loved him. He said he had no idea how he contracted the disease. I offered up the possibility of his first wife, who, according to him, was a drug abuser and cheated on him. He said he had walked in on her with another man and that's why he left.

Today I know the truth in my heart. He didn't get the disease from his ex-wife. He more than likely gave it to her. He died in 1995 and she died in 1999. I found out after his death that he knew he had the disease all along. I found out after his death that he and his mother had a plan—that he wouldn't die alone.

When he got out of the hospital, he used to say to me that we could move away, and when I got sick, we would take care of one another. He had this vision of us riding off into the sunset together. I had no plans of ever getting sick. God had another plan, another vision for my life.

I was certain from the moment that I heard he was infected that I was not. I don't know why I knew; I just knew that I was covered in the blood of Jesus and there was no way that I could be infected.

In the early 1990s the testing process wasn't as advanced as it is today. You had to wait several weeks for the results. I waited patiently because I knew. I prayed from the moment that I found out that God would spare my life and my health. I prayed. And then I relaxed in my faith. And sure enough, when the test came back, it said I was clear—no HIV virus was found anywhere in my system.

I believe that God had a plan for my life and that he wanted me to live to share my story, to inspire others, to be a living example of living a life of faith.

In my book, *Faith Under Fire: Betrayed by a Thing Called Love,* I go into detail about my life with this man—from contemplating killing him, to changing his diapers in his last days (yes, I stayed until the very end), to the drama with his family when he died (especially with one sister who was a culprit in hiding his secrets).

There are too many secrets in too many relationships in this world. Secrets kill. Lies kill. And there are women who think they are protecting the men in their lives—there are mothers, sisters, and wives who are hiding things for their men—but what they are really doing is destroying lives. The root of destruction of families today is secrets. It's time for people to stop lying and start telling the truth. And start living a life that is open and free.

His family used to make fun of me because of how

"clean" a life I led. I would always go to bed early and get proper sleep. I didn't eat processed foods or red meat. I ate a lot of vegetables to the point where they called me "rabbit." I didn't drink and I exercised and took care of myself. I know now that my lifestyle helped save my life—it strengthened my system and helped protect me from the disease that I was exposed to so many times.

I was supposed to survive so I could tell my story. In *Faith Under Fire: Betrayed by a Thing Called Love*, I talk about that journey, and much like *On the Up and Up*, it is a story of triumph.

For every tragic ending there is a story of faith and overcoming. Like Brenda, I was blessed to move on. I found the love of my life—my childhood sweetheart, who was supposed to be my husband from the beginning. We have a beautiful daughter and we share a love for Christ.

I am here today because of my faith. I had to fight through some very difficult barriers. The doctors were doubtful. How could I possibly be married to him for two years and not be infected? My family was worried beyond belief. Although they taught me about faith, they exhibited very little of it. They lost it. I was the only one who was saying, "Don't worry! I am not infected!" I was standing in the middle of the fire and I didn't even catch a single ember. I was unscathed.

When everyone wanted me to leave him, I stayed. I stayed until the end because that's how I would have wanted to be treated. You cannot fight evil for evil.

And what he did to me—that was his cross to bear, not mine. He would have to answer to that, not me. I'm God's girl.

The most valuable lesson I learned as a woman, as I walked through the fire and kept my faith, was that the Bible is a very good guide. I married a man who lied to me and died from AIDS because I wasn't obedient to the Word. I was out there *looking* for a man when the Bible is clear that it is a ". . . good man who *finds* a good woman." He is the one who should be looking, not me. And when I realized this later, and waited on God, I got more than I could ever have hoped for or expected. I got a perfect man for me.

LaJoyce Brookshire

Introduction

LIVING ON THE UP AND UP

"I'm sorry." Those were the words I was looking for. More than fifteen years had passed since our ugly breakup and subsequent divorce and all I wanted was an "I'm sorry." I wanted to know that it wasn't my fault. I needed to know that I wasn't crazy and those two simple words would have released me from years of self-doubt and anger.

My ex-husband, J.L. King, whom I have known only as Jimmy—my Jimmy—never apologized for what he did to me. In his book, *On the Down Low: A Journey into the Lives of "Straight" Black Men Who Sleep with Men,* he chronicled his life—our life together—when he discovered he liked having sex with men. While he was cruising the parks, going to those men-only parties and finding new "friends" right under my nose, he was living the life of the perfect husband and father. He gave the perfect picture of a family man—complete with two children and a fine home. He was a pillar of the community. He was successful. We attended church as a family. To the world, we were the quintessential family. But as Jimmy laid out in his book, that was one big lie.

Unfortunately, it was a lie that I, too, was forced to live because I did not know. And when I had an inkling of what he was doing and with whom he was doing it, I still had doubts. I doubted myself.

One Saturday night in 2002, I found myself in front of the television watching my ex-husband tell the world that he was a man living on the "down low." It had been several months since Jimmy invited me and our daughter, Ebony, over to share something "that will change all of our lives forever." Now I was sitting there actually looking at what he was talking about in color. And it hurt.

That night several months before, Jimmy called me out of the blue and said he had something to tell me and Ebony—something that would change our lives. He said he wanted to talk to us face-to-face and that he would talk to our son, Brandon, separately.

Ebony picked me up and we drove to Columbus to Jimmy's house, a brownstone in an upscale neighborhood. We went around to the back door. I had never been to his new house and I was impressed with how clean the kitchen was (I have always been partial to kitchens because I love to cook). The place had hardwood floors and was very well decorated. Jimmy always had that touch. He still has that touch. It's one of the few things I missed about him.

His house also had a nice, masculine feel. He had

rich leather furniture, brass tables, and statues and artwork of some famous black artists. We sat in the living room. He poured himself a glass of E&J and said to me, "I'd offer you one, but I know you don't drink."

That is true. I don't drink, and when I did, it was only socially to fit in with his crowd. I never liked the way alcohol made me feel, and I had one bad experience in college where I got violently sick after drinking with a friend that pretty much cured me of any taste I might have had for alcohol.

Jimmy poured himself a healthy glass and sat down on the couch and started to speak. He seemed nervous, which he rarely was. He even had a nervous smile on his face.

"What I brought you here for was to tell you something that is going to change all of our lives," he said dramatically.

"What could be so awful that it would change our lives?" I thought.

"With every good thing comes some negativity," he said.

He was fidgeting and fumbling. He was beating around the bush and I wanted to scream: "Just come on out with it already!"

He kept talking about how there are men who have sex with men and they are infecting women and how they aren't being honest about their lifestyle.

"Okay . . . but what about you?" I thought.

Ebony finally jumped in and said, "I don't understand what you're saying. What exactly are you saying? It's not clear."

Jimmy stumbled and stalled. He skirted around it. Ebony and I both already knew the truth. We had talked about it. But we wanted to hear him say it. We knew what he was trying to say, but we didn't let him off the hook.

He told us he would be speaking about the subject of men who have sex with men and would be touring around the country as an AIDS activist. I wanted to ask him if he had AIDS but I didn't. I didn't want to ask him in front of Ebony just in case. I didn't want her to know the answer if that answer was yes. And I wanted to hear the rest of what he had to say, which he would never get to if I dropped that bombshell question on him.

Jimmy continued to hem and haw and never once got around to admitting that he was actually one of these men who have sex with men that he'd be talking about around the country. He talked about the phenomenon and how he wanted to help save the lives of women but he never said, "I am talking about me."

After he finished, we exchanged pleasantries and we left. Ebony dropped me off at home and she went back to her apartment.

The next thing I knew I was watching Jimmy on television. He was being featured on a CNN special on men on the down low, or DL. To see him in color speaking so candidly about his "lifestyle" and his "desires" hurt. Here he was telling the world something he could never say to my face.

I thought I was long since over the pain that he'd caused through his lies and deception. But it stung me to see him on television before the world speaking about things that he still could not share with me.

As I sat there watching this "special" on CNN, it was difficult to put into words what I was really feeling. But the pain felt new—as fresh as the day that I put him out. In the midst of thinking about my own raw feelings, I thought about our children, Ebony and Brandon. I wondered if they were watching, too.

Ebony lives in Maryland and Brandon lives in another city in Ohio. I knew they were both grown, but as their mother, I still wanted to protect them from hurt or whatever other feelings they might have. I know that they both have a wonderful support system in their friends and coworkers, but it was still about their father.

Ebony is a schoolteacher and is naturally compassionate and has many friends. And Brandon, who is quieter than the outgoing Ebony, also has a tight-knit group of friends. I wondered what their friends would think and how Ebony and Brandon would explain it all. Then I got a little angry that they might even have to.

Here was their father—a man they'd grown up believing was a certain way—on national television exposing *his* secrets (which were really *our* secrets). What happened to Mama telling us, "Don't go telling your family business"?

That's the way I grew up and that's the way I basically raised my kids. Family business stayed in the family. Actually, that kind of business wasn't even discussed *within* the family. It just wasn't done. Now it was all out there. The whole CNN audience—which might as well have been the entire world—knew that my ex-husband cheated on me with men.

Then it got worse. The book came out. And it turned into a national sensation—twelve weeks in the top ten of the *New York Times* best-seller list. It became the subject of much debate—even a segment on *Oprah*.

Jimmy didn't even have the courtesy to make sure I got a copy of the book before it came out. He got the galleys, or uncorrected proofs, to Ebony because she was joining him on *Oprah*.

I was so mad, I didn't want to read it. Ebony tried to convince me to read it.

"Mom, he makes you look like a queen in this book," she said. "Let me read some of it to you." I told her not to but she read a little to me anyway. Again, I couldn't understand the things he was saying in the book. He was saying things I had never heard out of his mouth. Things he should have said to me a long time ago. I should have been the first one to read his book, since I was so prominently featured in it. I didn't want anyone to call me and tell me things that they read. I should have been the first one to review it because it was about me. There would be no *On the Down Low* if Jimmy didn't have me to be on the down low with. It was as much my story as it was his.

I finally decided to read it. And when I did, I was so relieved that I actually cried. I felt like he'd finally admitted what he had done to me. He admitted it not only to me, but to the world. And I thought, "This is my apology." He couldn't say it to me, but he could write it in a book.

Then I thought if he really felt that way about me, why didn't he try to change? Why didn't he either leave me alone from the beginning or change and make it better for us? I got angry about that, too. He messed up my life. When he wrote about us both being virgins, all I could think was, "Yeah, you stole my virginity! I trusted you with that. And you trampled on it!"

After I calmed down, I began to see the bigger picture. This wasn't about me at all. It was about the thousands, perhaps more, women who are still living with men who are on the down low. This is about their story and about saving their lives.

And as I searched my soul, I realized that the anger and the pain were just pent-up anger and pain that I had not been able to express so many years ago. It wasn't about having my dirty laundry aired for the world to see, because it wasn't really *my* dirty laundry; it was simply the first time I had a chance to release all that I was feeling.

They were the feelings I was never allowed to experience because for so many years I had been living a lie—stuffing away my feelings, pretending.

I had a lot bottled up and questions like "What if you are wrong?" haunting me. Because Jimmy never admitted it—never said, "Yes, Brenda, you were right. You caught me red-handed"—I could never really let it go. Even though I knew in my spirit and God had confirmed that I was right, our pastor's words, "Brenda, you don't want to accuse an innocent man," still chased me.

Because Jimmy never came clean to me, never came to me as a man, being one hundred percent honest, I felt robbed. I was robbed of the opportunity to truly grieve. When a husband dies, there is closure. When you catch your man sleeping with another woman, there is closure. You get support because society understands that—and somehow that is acceptable. You get to cry out loud and there are support groups and sister girlfriends who will rally around you.

But when you find out your husband was sleeping with a man, where do you turn? I turned to my church and was told that I was wrong for even accusing him. I had one good friend—my sister-in-law— who was there for me. But by and large, my family loved Jimmy. Even my brother John, whom Jimmy said he never liked, was one of Jimmy's biggest fans. In fact, he was his best man at our wedding. John had no idea Jimmy never liked him and didn't find out that fact until he read it in *On the Down Low*. I guess Jimmy was real good at hiding his feelings.

My own family never wanted to see him for what he really was. And for the sake of my children, I kept his secrets. I couldn't paint the true picture.

So I lied, too—mostly to myself. I went through denial. I sucked it all up, sucked it in, and put on a good front. Meanwhile, I robbed myself of the growth that should have taken place from absorbing all of the pain and then allowing myself to heal.

After reading Jimmy's book, I sat in that comfortable chair in the middle of my family, in the middle of winter, and I finally cried. These were the tears that I was holding back. I cried for the lost years that I gave to Jimmy. I cried for my youth that he stole. I cried for my virginity. For me, I was saving myself for my husband, whom I had envisioned being with until death do us part. But for him, I guess I was an experiment to see if he, in fact, enjoyed being with women.

I was robbed of my innocence and robbed of my ability to truly trust.

When I finished crying, I felt a tremendous burden lift. And while I could never get back all I felt had been taken from me, I could try to make sure that it didn't happen to any other woman. What Jimmy had done, bringing his story to the world—putting a real live face to all of those characters featured in E. Lynn Harris's novels—made the issue of men leading double lives a real phenomenon. It shattered many myths and broke a lot of lives. But no one was there to pick up the pieces for these women.

When I was able to think about my life with Jimmy and the times when I should have known, but was oblivious to the things he was really doing, I thought about my life being in jeopardy. How many times had he had sex with a man and come home and had sex with me? I could have contracted any number of diseases, including HIV and AIDS.

God delivered me from that situation. I could have been one of the women that they were interviewing with HIV on that CNN program—whose lives were completely ruined by the lies of their men.

Two simple words could have changed my life. "I'm sorry" would have sufficed for me. It would have validated everything. But Jimmy never uttered those words to me—and perhaps he never will. But his nationally best-selling book, his appearance on CNN, his many interviews in magazines like *Essence* and *Ebony,* and his appearance on *The Oprah Winfrey Show* in the spring of 2004 were an apology.

Jimmy finally admitted in great detail to the entire world that he had been having sex with men while married to me. I was not crazy.

And I thank him for finally admitting the truth. For more than fifteen years I carried his lie around with me like an old bag that I somehow couldn't part with—it wasn't serving its purpose anymore and it didn't look good, nor did it match my current wardrobe, but I just couldn't bring myself to throw it away. That old bag had some sentimental value, I thought. Or perhaps, in some ways, that old bag defined who I thought I might still be.

After his book came out, not only did I toss that old bag away, I torched it—burned it to a crisp so that not one trace of it remains. And I am free.

My name is Brenda Stone Browder and I am free from the anger, free from the hurt, and free from the shame that I carried around after discovering that the man that I married, the father of my kids, the love of my life, had been sleeping with men behind my back.

For years I kept all of those emotions inside while putting on a good public face. The circumstances behind our divorce in 1981 were not widely known. I didn't talk about them to many people. I didn't want anyone to know. I kept Jimmy's secrets for a number of reasons, which I will explore in this book. But perhaps the biggest reason why I kept silent for so long was because of what I felt the things that he was doing to me and to our family meant about me. I kept his secret because I didn't want to shatter the image that he had created for himself. But I really kept his secret because I didn't want to shatter *my* image.

I believed that his living on the "down low" meant that I was lacking in some ways as a wife and as a woman. Perhaps I didn't do something. Perhaps I didn't do enough to keep him from straying. Perhaps there was something wrong with me.

These are issues that women whose husbands cheat on them or leave them for another woman deal with.

These are the questions that women have in "normal" relationships. But my issues were compounded because I caught my man having an affair with another man. And for a while, I somehow felt that perhaps I wasn't woman enough.

Today, I realize that I *wasn't* woman enough for Jimmy. I was *too* much of a woman for him. Because the truth is that my womanhood or womanliness was not what he was seeking. And I could have been Halle Berry or the Queen of Sheba and Jimmy still would have done the things that he did.

His actions had nothing to do with me. What Jimmy did in deceiving me, our family, and in many ways himself was all about him. He was searching for answers. He was the one who needed to be true to himself.

Looking back, Jimmy probably never should have gotten married. But because we live in a society where a gay lifestyle is not accepted—especially in the black community—Jimmy never felt like he could openly explore the feelings he'd probably had since he was very young. But that's no excuse for what he did. That's no excuse for putting someone you love through years of hurt and self-doubt—not to mention the impact it had on our children.

It's no excuse but I understand. And one of the reasons why I am writing this book is to help other women understand. It took me a long time to get here. It took me a while to forgive Jimmy. That forgiveness, though, had to start with me forgiving myself. It started with me loving myself. And it ends with me knowing that God has a plan for our lives and nothing happens to us that we cannot both handle and learn from.

Living with Jimmy and this whole down low phenomenon has sent me on a spiritual journey, which has developed into a ministry where today I am helping other people come to grips with the truths in their lives and work toward overcoming their sins. I give workshops throughout the country in which I discuss my life and how I dealt with the knowledge that my husband—the man I thought I would spend the rest of my life with—not only ruined our family but also jeopardized my life by having sex with men outside of our marriage.

After every workshop there are a couple of women who hang around afterward. They want to talk to me privately. They want to share their stories when no one else is around to hear them. Many women tell me that they thought they were the only ones who had something like this happen to them and they thank me for letting them know that they are not alone. They talk about the shame and the stripping down of their self-esteem. And they talk about needing to heal.

Some of the women I have encountered talk about staying in their marriage with their husband, even after finding out that he has slept with another man. I don't judge these women. They have to do what they feel is right for them and for their family. And I understand. But women need to be armed with the truth. They need to know what they are facing, and more importantly, they need to know that they are not alone and that it is not their fault.

In *On the Down Low,* Jimmy writes: "Nothing will make a brother who likes to have sex with other brothers stop. I know that sounds harsh, but it's true. If a man enjoys sex with a man, there's not a woman alive who can compete with that desire, because, it's simple, *she's not a man.*"

On October 27, 2004, Oprah Winfrey had a show featuring men who were married and had cheated on their wives with men. On this program Oprah revealed that there are millions of American men who are gay *and* married. In fact, she said, there are two million married couples in America where "at least one partner was gay and living a lie." And of them 15 percent stay married.

In an attempt to explain why a man who knew he was gay would marry an unsuspecting woman one of her guests explained, "Women are for devotion, men are for sex." In other words, he wanted the companionship and the comforts that a woman brings to a relationship, but when it came to sex, he preferred a man.

If a man is cheating on his wife with men, that is something he would do even if his wife were perfect in every way. That is *his* problem, not hers.

It becomes our problem when we don't know and

are infected by a disease because of his lies. While many want to focus on the sensational aspect of this "down low" thing, the reason why it is so important that we start talking more openly about it across the country and across the world is because women are dying. Women are the largest growing risk group for new HIV cases worldwide.

In India, according to a 2004 published report, monogamous housewives accounted for more than 22 percent of HIV infection cases. "India, with four million known carriers, has the second largest number of HIV/AIDS patients after South Africa. The spread of the infection is attributed to low investment in public health infrastructure, high poverty levels, illiteracy and ignorance, strong gender biases, myths and taboos associated with the infection, and silence on sexuality."

Silence kills.

According to a 2004 *Sky News* article entitled "Chinese Blood Trade Blamed for AIDS Crisis," which was featured on Planned Parenthood's website, Chinese women are also the largest group of newly infected HIV cases: "Up to now, intravenous drug use is still the major transmission channel, while unsanitary blood selling from the mid-1980s to 1990s has affected farming regions in central China. But with the increase in promiscuity and widespread prostitution, heterosexual contact will replace drug injection as the major cause of HIV and AIDS infections," Shen Jie, deputy director of the China Disease Prevention and

Control Centre, was quoted by the Xinhua news agency as saying.

In sub-Saharan Africa, the epidemic's victims are increasingly young and female, according to a report released in 2004 by the joint United Nations Program on AIDS (UNAIDS). It reports that 8.6 million people between the ages of fifteen and twenty-four are living with HIV or AIDS in that region—of these, 5.7 million are young women!

A February 2004 article in the *New York Times* reported that teenage brides in some African countries are becoming infected with the AIDS virus at higher rates than sexually active unmarried girls of similar ages in the same areas. Young, *married* girls.

According to the World Health Organization (WHO), by the end of 2003, 19.2 million women were living with HIV/AIDS worldwide, accounting for 50 percent of the 40 million adults living with the disease.

More than 90 percent of all of those infections have been as a result of heterosexual intercourse. The rate of infection among older women—women forty-five years and older—accounts for 18 percent of AIDS cases reported to the Centers for Disease Control and Prevention (CDC). That means that women who have been in marriages for years—women who have thought that they were in monogamous relationships, women who are just like I was—are dying because their mates are not being honest about their sexual practices.

During the 2004 vice presidential debate, moderator Gwen Iffel put the issue on the map when she posed this question to Vice President Dick Cheney and Senator John Edwards: "Are you aware that African American women are thirteen times more likely to contract HIV?"

In New York, the largest city in the country, more than a quarter of all HIV/AIDS cases are in Brooklyn and more than 60 percent of them are minority women. If Brooklyn was a state, it would rank sixth in the nation of newly diagnosed HIV cases among women.

This is an epidemic.

And among black and Hispanic women, that number is even greater. Together black and Hispanic women represent 25 percent of all women in the United States, yet they account for more than 82 percent of AIDS cases in women.

I am writing this book for them.

Initially, I thought about it from a very self-healing perspective. I needed some answers, I needed to learn how to forgive, and I wanted to show that you can pick up the broken pieces of your life and build a new future for yourself. But I also believe that a woman must be armed with the truth for her own protection. This book is about healing but it is also about understanding and sharing as much as I possibly can to make sure that what happened to me won't happen to the next woman. And if it does, she will know that there is a way out of it and a way to overcome. I want to empower women with knowledge because knowledge is power. And I want to empower them with the truth because the truth will set them free.

In hindsight, I have perfect vision. I couldn't see it then because I wasn't really looking. Women have to go into their relationships with their eyes wide open, considering all of the possibilities.

I was so naive, so in love. Jimmy was my world. He was a good husband, a good father. He was attentive. He was a good provider. He made sure he met all of my needs. He always made me feel comfortable. He treated me like a lady. He was romantic.

But he was a liar. My life with him was a lie. He was living on the down low. J.L. King must be applauded for putting a human face to a very inhumane behavior. He must be applauded for having the courage to tell his story and let thousands of women know that they aren't crazy.

But now it's time to take what he started and where he brought fear and doubt, give women hope and understanding. I am grateful for my life with Jimmy. He taught me a lot. The most valuable lesson was that there is no higher goal than to live an honest life. There is no greater reward than to be true to yourself.

I have moved on and have married again to a wonderful man. We have been married twenty years, and while it hasn't always been smooth sailing (what marriage is?), it has always been on the up and up.

Chapter 1

WAS MY MARRIAGE A LIE?

I married Jimmy when I was nineteen years old—a very young nineteen years old. I was the youngest of eight children (my oldest sister died when she was three). And I was the baby in every sense of the word. There were four years between me and my next oldest sister, and my parents weren't quite expecting me. In fact, my sister is called "Baby Gail" to this day because she was supposed to be the last girl. Then along came Brenda.

My parents spoiled me. I used to tease my brothers and sisters because I never really got a whooping. I watched them and learned. Not only did my parents spoil me, but so did my siblings. Everyone was very protective of me. I wasn't even allowed to date until I was sixteen going on seventeen. And I couldn't go on a date alone—one of my brothers or sisters had to chaperone. I was very sheltered.

The Stones were a tight-knit group who went to

church together on Sundays and ate supper together every evening. My father worked very hard and my mother worked equally hard taking care of her brood. I never wanted to do anything to disappoint my parents and I prided myself on being a "good girl."

When I discovered I liked boys—which was way before I was sixteen and allowed to date—there wasn't much I could do about it. I just fantasized and dreamed of one day being swept off my feet and getting married and having a family, just like in the romances I saw on television.

I actually had a fantasy "wedding" when I was about five years old. My mother thought it would be fun to have a Tom Thumb wedding with the boy next door, who was also five. Both mothers had a ball planning the wedding day. I even had on a tiny white wedding dress and he had on a tuxedo. We had a cake and everything.

Unfortunately, my "groom" was not a willing participant. He was very upset and did not want to do it. His mother threatened him or something to go through with the ceremony, but when it came time for the "you may kiss the bride" part, my man ran off. He left me standing at the altar. Maybe this should have been my first sign not to look for that fairy tale. But I was too young to process it all or even really care.

I didn't have my first boyfriend until my junior year in high school. One of my female classmates handed me a note during homeroom. She didn't tell me who it was from. The note said, "I like you and I want to talk to you. Will you go with me?"

The note had no signature. I assumed it was from Robert because we had been making eyes at each other since school started that year. I thought he liked me. I definitely liked him. Robert was fine. He was bowlegged and light-skinned with hazel eyes. Those were in the days when light skin and light eyes were in.

We started going with each other. Our budding romance was relegated to school, recess, and after school when he would carry my books and walk me as far as the train tracks, which were several blocks from my home. He couldn't come to my home. My parents weren't having any boys over to the house then.

One afternoon as he was walking me home, Robert tried to kiss me at the train tracks. He got a little forceful and that was the end of our "relationship." I was a good girl and he had crossed the line.

A few weeks later, Jimmy finally worked up the nerve to approach me. He admitted that he was the one who sent me the note and told me that he thought I was very beautiful. He was a real gentleman, very well mannered, and he made me feel like a princess.

Jimmy didn't hang out with a large crowd and I liked that. He wasn't into many of the things high school boys are into like sports and being a player with a bunch of girlfriends. He was thoughtful. He liked to read and he was romantic—everything I had ever daydreamed about in a man.

He was the first boy I actually brought home to meet my parents. But it took a few months before I would allow him to meet them. I wasn't bringing just anyone home. He had to pass my test first and he did. We started dating and soon he was able to come over to my house and endure hours on my front porch, with my parents watching us the whole time. He was even okay with our chaperoned dates to the movies.

Somehow with all of those eyes on us, we managed to fall in love. And instead of going to college, Jimmy entered the military so that we could start our lives together immediately. He wanted to get married and he knew he needed to be able to provide for me and our future family. So as soon as he graduated, he enlisted—against his parents' wishes.

Jimmy went through basic training and was starting his military career. That next Christmas he gave me a beautiful engagement ring. We had actually gone window-shopping looking at wedding ring sets, and he surprised me with the set that I had fallen in love with. We were excited that we would be married, and planned on a June wedding. I had graduated from high school that May. I was in my freshman year at Central State University. The date that we picked was my parents' wedding anniversary, June 14.

I didn't say anything to my parents about how soon we wanted to get married because I thought they would object. In fact, I knew they would object.

They felt we were both too young. And at that time in Ohio, we would have needed our parents' signatures to marry before our twenty-first birthdays. Jimmy was twenty and I was nineteen. My parents wanted me to go to and finish college before getting married. They didn't say much about the engagement, but a wedding so soon would be a battle.

So I started to plan my wedding without anyone's input. I didn't even tell any of my sisters. I only told my niece, who was one of my best friends. She and I were the same age. I didn't want any flack from my parents or siblings. I put my engagement in the local newspaper, registered at a bridal registry at a major department store in my hometown, and picked out my china pattern, silverware, and glassware. I started collecting items for my trousseau, and I ordered my invitations. I did all of this on my own. I figured the main worry to my parents would be the cost of a large wedding, so I planned something quaint and simple, and most of all not costly.

It was amazing I was able to do so much on my own, considering the lack of funds. I was working at a 7-Eleven during my senior year. But my father made me quit. One evening a man came in the store yelling and giving everyone a hard time. Then he came straight for the cash register and tried to open it to take the cash out. I anticipated him doing this after I had witnessed his antics through the large, plate-glass window on the front of the store before he even came into the store.

There was a building under construction next door and the workers had left various pieces of lumber in the area for the evening. The belligerent man picked up a two-by-four and rammed it through a car parked in the lot. There was a toddler in the backseat. Luckily, no one was hurt. When I saw that, my intuition kicked in. I knew that he would be coming into the store bringing trouble with him. I was behind the counter waiting on customers at the time. I locked the cash register and took the key with me, then I walked nonchalantly to the back of the store and pretended to be a customer.

After he discovered he couldn't get into the cash register after pounding on it and trying everything he could think of, he left aggravated.

I didn't tell my father about the incident because he would have put his foot down and insisted that I leave. But I eventually quit a few weeks later when another customer grabbed my hand to look at my diamond engagement ring and said, "Ooh wee! Your man must really love you to give you a rock that big!" I thought he would try to take it off of my finger. I pulled my hand away as another customer came up to the counter and the man eventually left.

It was time for me to listen to my daddy. I quit. But I had made enough money to pay all of the deposits for my wedding.

We planned to have our ceremony on my parents' lawn; my parents had a beautiful backyard. Everything was going very well for me until my niece let the cat out of the bag. She told my father that I was making tissue paper flowers for an outside trellis for my wedding. My parents were upset when they found out that I had planned on marrying so soon after getting engaged and before I finished college. They objected and made me cancel my plans. They said that they would not sign for me.

In my mind, I just knew that if I had everything in order and even planned to marry on their anniversary that they could not object. They did not seem to have a problem with who I was marrying but that I wanted to get married so young. I argued that my mother was the same age when she and my father married, but they didn't want to hear it.

Jimmy was away in the service, stationed in upper Michigan, and I was determined to be with him one way or another. I wanted to marry just to be with him. So I was persistent. I kept pressuring my parents, and when I wasn't pressuring them to let me marry, I would mope around the house being miserable and making them miserable. They finally relented.

Then we had another problem—Jimmy's parents. Actually, his mother. She did not want her baby boy to get married. I don't think age was an issue for Mrs. King. I don't think she ever wanted Jimmy to marry— anyone. I don't think she believed any woman was good enough for her Jimmy. (Perhaps she knew something I didn't.)

June came and went and it was now September, near my birthday. We finally got Jimmy's parents to agree, too, and we planned for an October wedding. I made my wedding dress the night before, and my sisters helped decorate the living room and the rest of the house for our reception. It was too chilly to have a backyard wedding, so we opted for my parents' living room.

Our family and a few friends were present. Baby Gail was my bridesmaid, and my brother was the best man. Even Jimmy's mother—who threatened not to show up, despite signing the papers—was there. I heard she'd cried the entire night before. She showed up in an unattractive pants suit, and it seemed as though she thought, "I'm going to come, but I'm not going to look happy about it!" She sure didn't. But I tried to ignore her attitude and enjoy my special day.

I was happy, but terrified, to finally get married. I remember having second thoughts, thinking that I shouldn't do this because my parents didn't want me to. But the alternative would be staying and living in their house. That was scarier. I didn't want to be under my parents' rule anymore. I wanted to be grown, to make my own decisions. Little did I know, marrying Jimmy was like going into another controlling situation.

It was a beautiful ceremony. As we stood at the altar and the minister asked us to say our vows, Jimmy grabbed my right hand and slipped the ring on my right ring finger. I quickly pulled the ring off and put it on the ring finger of my left hand, hoping no one else noticed. But I got a weird (read: bad) feeling about him putting the ring on the wrong hand.

"Oh, I'm not really married," I thought. The ring was originally placed on the wrong hand; does that mean something? I was so upset. But like his mother's antics, I tried to ignore my feelings and put on a good face. I never said anything to Jimmy about it—at least not that day.

We went on with the ceremony and the party afterward. But you could see that I had a frown on my face in some of our wedding photos. I was still thinking about that ring being on the wrong hand.

As I think back on the ring incident now, I feel that it was definitely a sign—not only did he put the ring on the wrong finger, but he was also the wrong man for me. However, I wanted to be married. I was in love!

Most of our wedding night was like something out of a romance novel. We went to a local hotel, and stayed in the bridal suite. It was storybook-like. Jimmy carried me across the threshold. I remember the suite having a beautiful red heart-shaped bathtub. Jimmy did not want to waste time getting into the tub. So I just changed into my beautiful wedding nightgown that I had in my trousseau. I was so nervous and excited.

Jimmy broke the mood by telling me that my nightie looked like a shroud. I was hurt. I wanted to please him and he didn't like it. So I took it off and we made love all night. I was a virgin. He was a virgin. But it seemed like he knew exactly what he was doing.

When our honeymoon was over, Jimmy got an overseas assignment in Turkey. I had to stay in Springfield, and I was depressed. I was a married woman who didn't feel like a married woman. I did move out of my parents' house, though, and moved in with my sister and her husband. They were very welcoming and understood why I did not feel comfortable remaining in my parents' home after marrying. I still would have been their "little girl."

Jimmy had to stay on the base in Michigan for a month before shipping out. His father wanted to pay for me to go to Michigan so that I could live on the base with Jimmy. It was very cold in upper Michigan, and there was so little time until Jimmy was being shipped overseas that we decided that I would stay in Ohio at my sister's house.

He would come home on leave on the weekends and I would have our room perfect for him. I would have a bubble bath ready when he came through the front door. And we would make love all night and talk and catch up with each other.

When he was finally shipped out, he constantly wrote me letters and sent me cards proclaiming his love for me. I missed him dearly. I had enrolled in Central State and was going to please my parents and finish college. But I wanted to be with my husband.

In his letters and phone calls, Jimmy would express his desire to start a family. And I wanted nothing more than to have his babies. I found out in February that I was pregnant.

I found out the results while I was in school and I rushed to a pay phone in the student union to call Jimmy collect in Turkey. He was elated. I prepared to join my husband. Friends and family members tried to convince me not to go. But my place was with my husband. What was the point in being married if I couldn't be with him?

So I took my first plane ride ever—halfway around the world. The flight was seventeen long hours. I was pregnant, alone, and afraid, but I kept thinking, "I'm going to be with my husband!" And that made everything all right. I arrived at the airport and Jimmy was there to meet me. We then had to take a two-hour bus ride to our apartment in Izmir, Turkey.

He had already picked out our apartment, and made sure that we had room for a nursery for the baby. Now I began to feel like a married woman. We furnished our apartment; we had custom-made drapes and custom-made furniture. He let me pick out everything and he agreed with my choices. Everything was perfect. Even the pregnancy. I had very little morning sickness and no complications—except for a month before the baby was born, I broke out in hives on my thighs. I believe this was because I was nervous about giving birth without my family around.

Here I was in a strange country, with strange people, speaking a strange language, and I was about to give birth to my first child—no mother, no father, no sisters, no brothers. I was all alone—just me and my husband. Jimmy worked most of the day on the base, so I was alone. I struck up a friendship with our land-lady, who spoke very little English. She was a wonderful woman. We would exchange recipes and life stories as she taught me to speak a little Turkish and I taught her more English. I also befriended a woman I met on the bus, who was an English teacher from the United States. We would go shopping together and became very good friends. But most of my time was spent at home with Jimmy and his friends.

Jimmy had some friends from the base who would visit on occasion. He wanted me to join this military club that would meet for social gatherings, but the people seemed stranger than the native people from Turkey. I felt more comfortable with our landlady.

Two weeks prior to my due date, I had to take a two-hour plane ride to Adana, Turkey. There was no military base hospital in Izmir. I stayed in the "Stork's Nest" and waited for the birth of our first child. Jimmy could not take leave immediately, so I stayed there completely alone for one week. He came later and stayed in the Air Force barracks in Adana. He would come and pick me up from the Stork's Nest, which was more like a hotel than a hospital. We would talk, take walks, and make ceramics. Jimmy always enjoyed art. The night our baby was born, we had decided to go bowling—yes, bowling. I was still very active despite being pregnant. I had been a cheerleader while in high school, cheering for Upward Bound at Wittenberg University, and in college and kept in good shape.

After we had bowled a couple of games, I got tired

and Jimmy took me back to the Stork's Nest. I went to bed and woke up in the middle of the night to go to the bathroom. Well, I thought I had to go to the bathroom. Actually my water broke. I was not experiencing any labor pains, just discomfort. I went to the nurses' station around the hall and told them that I thought my water broke. They immediately examined me and found that I had already dilated enough for my baby to be born. They had no time to prep me or to give me any drugs, which I was thankful for because I wanted a natural childbirth. They only had time to call the doctor and Jimmy.

Jimmy got there before the doctor did. He was so excited. The baby came in less than an hour. And Jimmy was beaming at the sight of his beautiful little girl. I could tell he was very proud. So was I. But in addition to being a new mother, there were so many other adjustments for me. It was a little overwhelming with the baby in a foreign land with my husband spending a lot of time away from the home, with me not having any family and very few friends to rely on.

I must have had postpartum depression. For six weeks I was supposed to stay in the house with the baby and I was a mess. One evening Jimmy came home from work and I just looked at him and yelled, "Take me out of this apartment! I can't stand it! Take me somewhere!"

So he packed up Ebony and her things, and we took a bus ride to the end of the bus line and came back home. I was okay by the time we got back. I think Jimmy thought that he needed to get me out of that apartment and take me anywhere before I lost my mind. And he was right.

He knew how homesick I was. After my "breakdown" (keep in mind that I never raised my voice, let alone yelled, at Jimmy so for him it must have seemed like I was having a breakdown), he did everything he could to keep me occupied.

Jimmy started taking me places. We went to Ephesus, ancient city ruins, a city in the Bible where Paul wrote some of his letters to the church and where the Book of Ephesians originated. Jimmy also took me to the Black Sea. Ebony was about nine months old then. We had so much fun wading in the crystal clear water with her.

When I first got to Turkey, I didn't like it much. But I was finally starting to feel comfortable. It wasn't home, but I felt a lot better about being there.

Jimmy and I made friends with a Turkish couple in the building. They were both English teachers. They took us around to various historical places, such as the House of the Virgin Mary, where Jesus' mother reportedly lived.

We were finally settling into living in Turkey. We were on our way to being the dream family we used to talk about.

Then Jimmy brought home a friend he'd met on the base from Texas, and things took a turn for the worse. This newfound friend, whom Jimmy grew to view like a brother and I grew to view as an intruder, created a wedge in our relationship, which I will discuss in detail later. It always seemed as though just as things were going smoothly in our relationship, something or someone would happen to mess it up, to bring chaos.

It was his friend Paul who caused the most pain in my life at this time. And he was the reason why, when Jimmy was released from his duties overseas and had an opportunity to move back to the States, he chose to move us to San Antonio, Texas. That's where Paul was from.

After two years in Turkey, I was excited about going home—but I was not happy about moving to Texas. We stayed in Ohio for two weeks to visit our families. We'd had our household items shipped to Texas already so we didn't have to worry about our things. We stayed at Jimmy's parents' house before moving to Texas. It was a very sad time for me. I didn't want to leave home—Ohio. And I definitely didn't want to move to the same town with the man who had been such a huge pain for me in Turkey. It was unfair, but Jimmy wasn't listening to me. That's what he wanted to do, so that's what we did.

Contrary to what I expected, our move to Texas wasn't so bad after all. We ended up making a few friends besides Paul. And we started to entertain at our home and do things with other couples.

We went on a camping trip with two other couples, one of which had a little boy around the same age as Ebony. The men fished, the women cooked on an open fire, and the children played. It was a blast. We would have picnics and throw card parties. Texas was becoming fun for me.

We had one house party that was so wild, the next morning I got up and the bartender we'd hired for the evening was asleep on our living room floor. The bartender was actually one of my workers from the local Circle K convenience store, which I managed. He had ridden over on his motorcycle and, while he was bartending, apparently was also partaking of the alcohol himself and was too drunk to drive home. He must have tried unsuccessfully because I discovered his bike laying on its side in the yard leaking gas.

It was a nice motorcycle. He gave me my first motorcycle ride on it. He also rode me home a couple of times on it when Jimmy was supposed to pick me up and didn't show. I trusted him after that ride because he knew I was afraid. I remember him telling me, "Lean into the curves!" That was why we let him in our home to bartend. I trusted him. He was also my best and most reliable employee. He'd just had a bad night.

When he woke up, he was so upset with himself and very embarrassed. But I didn't care. He was still cool with me.

It was a very happy time for us. My parents, sister, niece, and nephew even came to visit us. And we showed them the time of their life.

Jimmy and I had been married for four years. We had a beautiful daughter and a nice life. Then I got the news that I was pregnant. What more happiness could we have? We were both pleased about the pregnancy. Ebony was almost four, and we felt she needed a sibling. I always wanted a large family. I came from a large family, and I wanted Ebony to experience having brothers and sisters, too. I had even talked to Jimmy about adoption. He was against it.

When I found out I was pregnant, I couldn't wait to tell him. And he seemed just as excited as I was. We were pretty stable financially so we could afford another child. I was the manager at Circle K, and Jimmy was moving up in rank in the Air Force. We didn't have to worry about health-care costs.

I was health conscious with this pregnancy as I was with Ebony. I exercised, ate right, and was careful not to put Tylenol in my system. I began to gain weight quickly. I was 110 pounds after having Ebony, but eventually went back to my high school weight of 125. I felt better with a little weight on my bones. I had become anemic with Ebony. The only difference was that I worked during this pregnancy.

There was nothing that I wouldn't do in my convenience store. It was spotless, just like my home. I would stock the shelves, mop, wash windows, keep the cooler stocked, even sweep the parking lot. If my help didn't show, I would take that shift and perform their duties as well as my own.

I got really big, really fast during this pregnancy. I saw my doctors regularly. My doctors' visits were demeaning. The way the base hospital cared for the servicemen's wives, and the servicewomen who were pregnant, left a lot to be desired. We all had what seemed like the same appointment on the same day. I felt like I was at a crowded meat market where you have to take a number and wait to be called. My number was my husband's social security number. And I felt like a number, not a pregnant mother.

I never saw the same doctor twice. They rotated the doctors and you had to see whoever was on duty at the time of your appointment. It was so impersonal. No one got a chance to get to know you, and they didn't get to know your case either. Each doctor would read your chart at your appointment. There was no chance to build a real doctor-patient relationship because you never knew who your doctor would be when you showed up for an appointment.

For the first few appointments—all of which were at Lackland Air Force Base Hospital—Jimmy went with me. In my seventh month, Jimmy could not take off work to go with me to my appointment. For the first time, I had a female doctor. She checked my chart and I went through the usual checkup. After listening to the heartbeat of my baby, which was routine, the doctor pulled the curtain and called another doctor to come in and listen. I was lying on the examination table wondering, "What's going on?!"

After the other doctor listened, they both left the room without saying a word to me. As they were leaving, I overheard the female doctor say something about "them."

"What do you mean, 'them'?" I asked.

It was like I was not in the room. She came back in and told me that they had heard the heartbeat and it was healthy and that I should come back in two weeks. During the next two weeks, the baby felt like he was trying out for the United States Olympic soccer team. He kept kicking and kicking.

"Either this baby has four arms and four legs, or there are two babies in there," I told Jimmy. He didn't pay much attention to me. He just smiled, humoring me.

I didn't make it back to that next appointment. One day while working at the store, I had been stocking the cooler with milk on the shelves and lifted a milk crate. I felt a twinge in my back and thought nothing of it. That night I awoke to severe pain. I shook Jimmy awake and told him that something was wrong. He was so alarmed that I was in such pain that he quickly called Paul and his wife to come over to get Ebony. There was no time to take her to their house. I needed to get to the hospital right away.

When we arrived at the hospital, they immediately took me into the emergency room and began to prepare me for my seventh-month baby to be born. Jimmy and I were both extremely worried, and I was in severe pain. Jimmy was at my side. Our baby was born quickly. I was still in pain. Then I heard the doctor yell for another incubator. I was in shock. I then understood that we were having twins. Jimmy was in shock, too.

The pain was excruciating. I remember yelling, "Get it out!" I thought it was the afterbirth that was giving me such pain. We were experiencing so many emotions, and physically my strength was drained. But there were two babies. Two baby boys.

They were so tiny. One weighed one pound two ounces and the other was one pound six ounces. They were so helpless. I remember looking at them in their incubators afraid to touch them for fear of hurting them. That first time touching them, as it turned out, would be my last.

Little Jelani Akil lived a day. Ebon James died the day after. I didn't know what to feel. I requested to be released from the hospital but the doctors wanted me to stay after both twins had died. That was too painful. I was in a room with two other women whose babies survived. I had to watch as they held their babies, fed their babies, loved their babies. It was the emptiest I had ever felt in my life. I didn't envy those women as much as I ached for my own babies. I wanted my little Jelani and Ebon to have lived.

When I returned home from the hospital, Ebony asked me, "Mommy, where are the babies?" My friend had told her that I had twins but had not told her that they had died. I told her that they didn't make it. She was sad. For her four-year-old mind, she seemed to understand. I had almost finished a blanket that I had begun to crochet for the baby/babies. I cut the yarn where I had stopped and gave it to Ebony. It was made of a soft, yellow baby yarn, with a metallic-like thread running through it. I gave it to her to wrap her baby dolls in, and she was so happy to have it. She still has that blanket.

Jimmy and I grieved together, supporting each other. He really took it hard. Jimmy told me that he cried all the way back from the hospital when he found out both twins had died. And I cried the whole day, too.

"Every man wants a son," he told me. "I had twin boys, two sons, and they both died."

We felt that we both needed our families back home in Ohio so we had the twins' bodies shipped to Ohio to be buried at home. We had to wait a week to have the funeral and burial because Ohio had a blizzard and the cemetery roads were impassable and the grave could not be opened because of the weather. My sister bought a white blanket for them to be wrapped together. They were too small for clothes. I wanted them together.

My mother was concerned about me. She wanted me to slow down and give my body and my spirit time to heal and to really grieve. But my way of dealing with it all was to keep busy. I had to keep moving because I didn't want to feel what I now know I should have allowed myself to feel.

As soon as a doctor gave us the okay, Jimmy and I decided to have another baby. I got pregnant again just a couple of months after losing the twins. Jimmy was extremely attentive during this pregnancy. He didn't want any problems or complications. He didn't even want me to work.

Almost a year after losing Jelani and Ebon, James Brandon was born. Jimmy had his baby boy. He has turned out to be such a blessing!

Chapter 2

I'M NOT CRAZY!

. . . To Melvin.

That was the name on the inscription of the jewelry Jimmy had purchased. I found the receipt after riffling though his billfold one evening while he was taking a bath. That inner voice, the one that tells you when things aren't right, had been talking to me like an old girlfriend—loud and steady. When I stopped ignoring that voice, I started investigating my husband.

As I stared at the receipt, my mind went numb. I don't even remember the rest of the engraving from this fancy jewelry store a few towns over in Yellow Springs, Ohio. All I remember was the name: Melvin. I stood there trembling in our bedroom unable to focus on anything. I couldn't think straight. But I knew. I knew that the voice that had been telling me something was wrong was very right. I had some answers but even more questions.

Why was Jimmy buying jewelry for Melvin? Was this really what it looked like?

My final question was, "Who will believe me?"

Who would believe that my husband, who was *the* man in our small town, was carrying on an affair with another man? Who would believe that my church-going husband, the perfect husband and father, son of one of the most prominent deacons in our town, was buying jewelry for a man instead of his wife? Who would believe that this perfect, happy household was bearing a nasty little secret?

When I was a young girl, I made a promise to myself that I would "save" myself for the right man, for my husband. And when I met Jimmy, I knew he was that man. Our courtship was something out of a fairy tale. Our marriage was perfect. He was perfect.

On my twenty-fifth birthday, Jimmy threw a surprise party for me at an upscale San Antonio restaurant. I thought we were just going for dinner, but when I arrived, all of my closest friends and family were there sitting around the table. It was an evening that I will never forget. It ended with a box and a huge diamond ring.

I could never imagine that four years from that wonderful night I would be standing in our bedroom holding a receipt for jewelry for someone else—a man named Melvin.

I had met Melvin a couple of weeks prior to finding the jewelry. Jimmy insisted that I meet Melvin. Actually, Jimmy had gotten busted and I now know that he was trying to cover his tracks.

I had recently started working at a children's home in our town. It was difficult for me to get a job when we relocated back to Springfield. Jimmy put a lot of pressure on me to get a job because money was tight after he was discharged from the Air Force.

Jimmy had a very good job at International Harvester, a truck manufacturing company. But the money and the cost of living weren't the same in Springfield.

I enrolled in the CETA program, a government agency that assisted minorities in securing employment. My first job was with the American Red Cross, which ended after eighteen months when the CETA employment funding ended. But that job led to a position as a youth leader with the Family and Children's Services (welfare department) at the Children's Home. I worked all three shifts there.

During this time, I was working the night shift, which ended at eleven. Jimmy had been staying home with the kids while I worked. One evening I got off earlier than usual and decided to take a different route home. I don't know why; I just did. Sometimes you are led to do things and you don't know why.

I took a back street to our home and passed by a local nightclub. As I was riding by, I noticed Jimmy's car parked out front. I couldn't imagine why he would be there, but it was definitely his car. The beat-up mustard-colored Cutlass was unmistakably Jimmy's. It was the only one in town.

I didn't stop. I continued home to find my nephew babysitting. He said Jimmy had called him to come over, saying he had some business to take care of. That night Jimmy came in about an hour after I got home. I asked him where he was. I didn't let on that I saw his car. He said he was out at a friend's house, something to do with the church singles ministry. I told him that I saw his car parked in front of the club.

"Oh," Jimmy said. "He lives next door to the club. In fact, I want you to meet him. He's good people."

I went that next night to meet Melvin. When I stepped into his home, the first thought I had was, "This man is a homosexual." It looked like a woman had decorated it. It was beautiful and tasteful and very feminine. And so was Melvin. He was typically handsome—light-skinned, green eyes, and curly hair. But he had a very soft air about him.

If I had suspicions before this night, they were confirmed.

And I had had my suspicions about Jimmy in the past. But each time I had questions, Jimmy was there to clear them away. Like the time I woke up in the middle of the night when we lived in San Antonio and I was looking for Jimmy, who had not come to bed. I discovered him in his "office," his special room in the house that was basically off-limits to me and the kids.

This was his place, his domain, where he conducted his business. He had picked out the furniture for this one room and decorated it himself.

One evening I had gone to bed early. I fell asleep, and when I woke up in the middle of the night, I turned over and to my surprise Jimmy still hadn't come to bed. I got up to find out what my husband was up to. I stood outside his "office" and I heard voices. It sounded like Jimmy was reading a book out loud or something, but the way he was reading it was very suggestive. I cracked open the door and poked my head in, and there I found Jimmy and Paul. They looked shocked to see me—in fact, they both practically turned white.

Jimmy got mad and asked, "What are you doing here?!"

"When are you coming to bed?" I asked.

"I'll be there when I get there," he barked. "Now go back to bed!"

And I shut the door and went back to bed. I lay there and cried myself to sleep. Jimmy never came to bed that night. And I'm not sure if Paul ever left before morning.

That evening should have been the end. But it wasn't. I convinced myself—as I had always done—that there was a reasonable explanation for Jimmy's actions. I pretended, at least to myself, that it must be my imagination. But as I stood in Melvin's home, in his presence, I could no longer deny what I was feeling.

Something was up with him and Jimmy. I knew it. And this time, I couldn't just ignore it. I had to do something.

After meeting and seeing Melvin face-to-face, I knew that he was a homosexual: His neat appearance, his particular ways, his mannerisms, his decorated home, his eyes—they all screamed "Homosexual!" And as I started to think back, Melvin wasn't the only "friend" of Jimmy's who was questionable.

When we came back from Melvin's house, all hell broke loose. I unleashed my findings—the jewelry receipt, which I had discovered just a couple of days before, the nude pictures he had taken by another man that he gave me before we moved back to Springfield, the blue boy magazines that I found in his closet the week before, the missing-you-badly letters from Paul from Texas that I didn't think much about until now, and the phone calls from strange men with high-pitched voices. It all came together for me and I confronted Jimmy about all of the "good people" he'd had around him during our eight years of marriage. I even confronted him about our fizzling sex life and his recent unusual request for anal sex. It all painted an ugly picture for me that I needed him to make sense of.

All of this came out in one big, nasty argument in our bedroom. I was crying. He was crying. We needed help. All I knew was that I needed out. The relationship was poisoning me. And I was scared. I felt betrayed and stripped of everything I had believed in. It wasn't fair.

After realizing that my husband had been cheating on me with at least one man, everything finally made sense. I understood that Jimmy did not want a woman. He really wanted to be with a man.

Once that sank in, I wanted to get as far away from Jimmy as I could. I was afraid because he was a whole different person to me. I no longer trusted him. He had changed. Perhaps I was seeing the real him for the first time.

I wanted out. I wanted a divorce. That was the only way to get away from him. He "owned" me. I felt that I had to do it immediately, or get caught in his web.

Every minute I spent around him confused me. His denials weakened me. He kept making me feel crazy, like I was making it all up. And believe it or not, despite the mounting evidence, I almost doubted myself.

I finally told him that if he could be honest and admit to the evidence, maybe we could get help and mend our relationship and keep our family intact. But he continued with the lie. "It's not true!" he said. "It wasn't me."

I told him that I loved him but that I loved my kids and myself more. I couldn't live with him anymore, not trusting him. There were so many lies. And the night of the big confrontation was it. It all came crashing in around us. I knew it was over and that I would have to start over. I had to begin my life again without him, as much as it hurt. I had no choice.

"I can compete with another woman," I told him. "But I cannot compete with another man."

I now know that to be so true. Looking back, I did not have what he wanted. I didn't have the right equipment, the right mentality, to keep him satisfied. At the height of our argument, Jimmy tried to convince me I was wrong by trying to make love to me. I was repulsed by the attempt.

"Get away from me!" I screamed. "Leave me alone!"

There was no way that I had any desire to make love to a man that I suspected of having sex with a man. I confronted Jimmy. I wanted to know why he had yet another homosexual friend in his life, why he had to have homosexual friends so close and spend time with them when he should be with his family.

He insisted there was nothing wrong with the friendships that he had. He always said that his friends were "good people." I then confronted him about the jewelry that he had engraved. I yelled at him, "Why do you need to give this man jewelry!" Just like the song "It Wasn't Me," Jimmy said, "I didn't buy anyone jewelry!"

"How can you tell me straight to my face that you didn't buy him jewelry?" I yelled. "I am not dumb. I have the receipt in my hand!"

He was incredulously still sticking to his lies. I told him that I couldn't live with his lies any longer. He had to go. I wanted our marriage to end. I even confronted him about his close friendship with Paul. He tried to tell me they were just close like brothers, that he loved him like a brother. I didn't want to hear any more lies. He made me sick. I told him to get out.

Jimmy ran down the stairs and jumped in his car and sped away like he had lost his mind. In the midst of all of the anger, I was still thinking about him. I was afraid for him. I called his parents' house and told them that he was behaving erratically and to be on the lookout for him.

His parents tried to calm the situation. I allowed him to come back home that night, but I stayed on my side of the bed and dared him to cross the line. The next day I was tormented coming to grips with my husband's infidelity and secret life. I insisted that we speak with our pastor to get counseling. He wouldn't go.

I was still going through the motions while in a daze about what was actually happening to our marriage. My life was crumbling. The picture-perfect couple that existed in my mind was becoming a nightmare. Jimmy was not acting at all like Jimmy, and I didn't know how to act because he had defined me. All I knew was that this was no way to live. I needed to do something, to make some changes for my well-being, and the well-being of the children. I tried to let them spend as much time with my family as possible so they would not see or feel what was going on in our home. As much as I tried to shield them from our drama, it was only a matter of time before they felt the strain.

The next day, Jimmy and I had taken a ride downtown to pay a bill. I began confronting him again. I couldn't let it go. "So tell me the truth about these friends of yours," I said. "All of these 'good people' that you hang around. What's the truth?!"

He got angry and began yelling at me, still denying the nature of the "friendships." I couldn't take it. He stopped at a stoplight about two blocks from our church. I pushed open the door, jumped out of the car, and ran to the church. I knocked on the pastor's office door. He invited me in after seeing my state.

I had never really had a conversation with our pastor before, but I knew I needed counseling and he seemed like someone who could help. We had been to his house on occasion, and his wife and I were friendly. I was so confused with everything that was going on that I needed some guidance. I needed someone to tell me what I should do. I went into the pastor's office, and I didn't know where to begin.

So I just blurted out, "I think my husband is having an affair with a man."

The pastor looked at me and didn't say anything at first. His expression didn't really change, but I could see that he was slightly annoyed.

"That's quite an accusation, sister," he said. "Are you sure?"

I told him about the jewelry and the time he was spending with one man in particular.

"That doesn't necessarily mean that he is having an affair," my pastor said. "In fact, it may not mean anything at all. I suggest you go home and try to be a better wife to your husband and pray for him and for your relationship. See what you can do to make things better."

See what *I* can do?

Then he said, "Sister, what if you are accusing him falsely? Think about that. What if what you think is going on, really isn't? How would you feel falsely accusing him? How can you make that up to him?"

I knew I wasn't wrong. But then I really started doubting myself. What if I was wrong? What if it was all in my imagination? I was completely dejected and confused after seeing my pastor. I was lost and felt very alone.

I went home and tried to process everything, including what the pastor had said. I tried to put on a good face and tried to keep it together. I cooked dinner, got the kids ready for bed, and I went to bed. I was a zombie. The next day was Sunday and we got up early.

It was summertime and I put on my black-and-white-striped dress—my favorite dress—stockings, and a hat. I looked good. I wanted to look extra good because I felt so bad inside. The kids looked perfect and Jimmy was dressed to impress, as always. We went to church looking like the perfect family.

I don't remember the morning service. I know we sat in our usual pew as a family. I remember that Jimmy's mother was there, the way she had always been. I knew that the pastor preached as he always did. I don't remember much else. After service, we went to his mother's. But I couldn't stay. I was called back to church. I had to go back to church.

While we went to church every Sunday, we did so more out of appearances than any real connection to God and Christ. I would go because that's what you do—that's what I always did. My parents went to church and that was part of my experience growing up. Jimmy's parents were prominent in their church. His father was a deacon. And his mother was very active. We were active in our church. But church was more social than spiritual.

On this day, however, I was compelled to go back for something more. I attended the afternoon service. Jimmy and the kids went to his mother's house. And I went back to church. I sat near the front of the church. I don't know what I was looking for exactly, but I wanted to hear from God. I was totally tuned in to what God would say to me. I asked for answers. That was the first time in my life that I felt the presence of the Holy Spirit.

The pastor called for us to pray. We were praying

in the pews, and the pastor called for people who wanted to be prayed for to come up. I wanted to go, but I had already talked to the pastor, and what could he say to me at altar call? This was between me and God at this point.

As people were going up to the altar, I noticed a man walk from behind me toward the altar. He was crying and speaking loud. I was close to the altar, close enough to see everything. The man stood right in front of me and started testifying.

"Lord," he said. "I've done wrong. I have broken up a home. Please forgive me!"

I looked up and it was Melvin—the man my husband had purchased jewelry for at an out-of-town jeweler. The man I knew my husband was sleeping with. I was shocked to see him. I was more shocked to see him go to the altar. But I felt this warm glow come over me. I knew God was giving me an answer, and in that moment I knew I wasn't wrong. I knew I was not the one who had broken up our marriage or accused Jimmy of something that was false. This was not my fault. God had given me the answer.

As I was praying and asking for an answer, Melvin was testifying and crying. He was distraught. He had a heavy heart. I should not have been able to hear what he was saying at the altar, but I could hear every word. That's when I knew this was a divine answer, and that's when I knew what I had to do.

"Forgive me, Lord," he said, crying hard. "I have sinned. I have broken up a family!"

I knew God had sent me a definitive answer. I knew the truth. I knew that I wasn't crazy.

I had not told a soul in my family about what was going on between me and Jimmy. I didn't tell anyone—except for my pastor—what I suspected. I was afraid. I felt like no one would understand—after all, who else was going through this? I felt like I was all alone.

And while I knew what I had to do—leave Jimmy— I wasn't sure how. Actually, I wasn't sure if I could. It hurt more that I had to do it. It would have been easy to stay. It was harder to do what I had to do. This was my first love. He was next to God for me. Whatever he said was right, was always right in my eyes. I trusted him with everything. Now I had to face the truth—all of that was a lie. Maybe I never wanted to see the truth. Maybe I knew the truth all along and needed to be slapped with it to wake up. But I was fully awake now.

That Monday while Jimmy was at work, I began to make my move. The first call was to a lawyer. I looked in the Yellow Pages for a divorce lawyer, and I called the first one I saw and made an appointment for the next day. Then I called my sister-in-law. She was the first person I told. She had always been my confidante. I then told my brothers. They couldn't believe it. There were no signs. It was really hard for them because they really liked Jimmy. And for years after, maybe until his book came out, some of my brothers were thinking, "I don't know if it's true." But despite their doubts, they rallied around me.

My adult nephews stayed with me while the locks were changed. The kids were staying with my brother and sister-in-law. I didn't want them in the middle of the mess that was unfolding. For them, it would be one big sleepover with their cousins. They didn't have a clue.

I packed up a few of Jimmy's things. I had become very good at packing, since we had moved so much. I made sure he had the things he needed and his bag was ready for him at the door when he came home. Two of my brothers were also waiting for him at the front door of our home—the beautiful home that we were supposed to grow old together in.

I heard Jimmy shouting through the cracked door, trying to talk to me. But my brothers stood in his way. He grabbed his stuff, jumped in his car, and sped off down the street like a crazy man. That night I cried for what seemed like forever. And some days when I think about my life with Jimmy, I still cry.

Chapter 3

PICKING UP THE PIECES

One of the hardest things I had to do after leaving Jimmy was carry on. Those first few weeks were so hard. I didn't know what to do. I was afraid. I didn't know how to survive by myself. I had gone straight from my parents' home into my home with Jimmy.

Jimmy had been my provider. I worked basically to add to the income for things we wanted. But he provided us with the things we needed. He took care of most of the household business such as the mortgage and paying all of the bills. He made repairs. I knew how to do things, but he was the one who actually did them. It was a major readjustment.

Jimmy was also a good father to our children. Now that role would be mine on a day-to-day basis. I would have to take care of our home. I was going to have to take care of our kids.

I had one thing going for me—I was a planner and

very organized. And I had a solid family behind me. So I got organized and turned to my family for help.

Jimmy wasn't making the transition go smoothly. He didn't want the divorce. But I think he didn't want to be the man whose wife left him. He didn't like the way it made him look. Maybe he really thought he wanted to be married. I believe he liked the idea of being married and the appearance of being married more than the marriage itself.

He started doing some crazy things. The first night after I changed the locks, I was getting ready to go to bed. My sister-in-law was with me. She stayed with us a lot during those first few weeks. She was still downstairs, and as I was heading to my bedroom, I noticed that the door was almost closed shut. I remembered leaving it wide open. I cracked it open and stepped inside, and Jimmy jumped out of the closet wearing nothing but his underwear and a pair of boots. He scared me pretty badly, and my sister-in-law came running upstairs after hearing me scream. I am glad she was a witness because no one would have believed how crazy he was that night.

I asked him to leave and he did. He had gotten in the house through my son's bedroom window. He'd apparently climbed in through the balcony. And he kept coming back into the house. The next week, I came downstairs to make breakfast for the kids and there was a note on the kitchen table that read: "You can't keep me out if I want to come in." He was coming in through the basement window, too.

Jimmy was out of his mind, which made me feel better about my decision but it also made the transition that much more difficult.

He had moved in with his parents temporarily, and the kids would go over there to visit him on the weekends. It wasn't that much of a break in routine for them because they spent most weekends at their grandmother's house anyway. On one of those visits he gave Ebony a rose—a black rose—to give me.

She said, "Dad said this is for you."

Thank God she had no idea what this meant.

He was trying to make me feel like I was the evil one. He was going around town telling people that I was the problem, that I was the crazy one who put him out for no reason.

During this time he made a trip to Texas and told our friends there that I had broken up the marriage. He was saying some crazy things about me. I found out because I called a few of our friends and they told me the things he was saying. I simply said that Jimmy was lying, and I never told them the truth about what happened. But I'm sure a few of his male friends already knew because they were up to the same tricks as Jimmy. They were in on it. Paul and all of those other friends were down with what Jimmy was doing because they were doing it, too. They were coconspirators—keeping each other's secrets.

I started thinking about Paul and how close he and Jimmy were and how they acted around each other and couldn't seem to spend enough time together, and

I started putting one and one together. And I remembered the way Paul used to treat his wife. He was horrible to her. She was such a kind, beautiful woman. She had started putting on weight, and Paul would humiliate her in front of people.

She would come to me crying so many times about the things Paul would say and do to her. I now know he was treating her that way because of the things he was doing behind her back. He was abusive to her because she was in the way.

Paul was a real trip. After he found out that Jimmy and I were divorcing, he had the nerve to ask me if I would move to Texas and live with him. He had just divorced his second wife by then. I told him he must be crazy. And Jimmy was acting just as crazy. He told me that someone had put a curse on me.

I believe he was acting out because he couldn't believe that I was finally standing up for myself. He didn't really allow that. He felt like I was his possession, that I was *his* wife and I should take him back. He was used to me acting in my normal way—anything he did or said was okay with me. But I asserted myself. I realized that he was not the person I married. That was my fantasy. That person that I thought he was, whom I had created in my own mind, probably never existed. This Jimmy was a complete stranger.

After I filed for divorce, he started getting really nasty. He demanded custody of the kids, which I was vehemently against. Then he wanted them for the entire summer. I was against that, too. Those were my babies, and I was still mad at Jimmy and didn't think he deserved to have the children for the entire summer. But my sister-in-law sat me down and said, "Brenda, he's just bluffing. He won't keep the kids for the whole summer. Watch." I agreed and she was right. It was rare that Jimmy would keep the kids for more than a couple of weeks, let alone the entire summer.

Despite the lies and the craziness, though, I still felt protective of Jimmy. While he was spreading lies about me, I was covering for him. Something inside me wanted to protect him. I still loved him and I didn't want other people to think badly of him. I wanted people to continue to respect him. It wasn't so unselfish, because I also felt if people thought badly about him, they would think badly about me.

It didn't do anything for my self-esteem to keep his secrets. In fact, it made me feel bad. But I had decided not to retaliate because whatever I did would be worse. I couldn't play the game the way he was playing it. I wasn't a mean-spirited type of person. I couldn't even think of the things he was doing.

Instead of dying inside, I did what I did as a kid when I was having problems—I ran to my father. This time, however, it was my Heavenly Father that I turned to. I began to turn to God and pray. I found comfort in the Word.

A woman from my church came over to visit me

during this time. She had just lost her husband to cancer the same month that I was divorcing Jimmy. They were a perfect couple. They were always together and seemed so happy. She came to me to comfort me and to get comfort.

"I think both of us are suffering a loss," she said. "We can be there for each other."

But I was thinking, "Mine is a different loss."

Her loss was an act of God. My loss was my man acting up. My loss was avoidable. At that point I stopped feeling sorry for myself and started getting angry with Jimmy. He ruined our marriage. And he broke my trust in a way I wasn't sure would ever be repaired.

It wasn't the cheating. I think we could have survived the cheating. Yes, I believe I could have eventually forgiven Jimmy for cheating on me—even with a man. I believed in "until death do us part." Our parents—both sets—stayed together through hardships. I felt like Jimmy and I could have survived this but he wasn't willing to tell the truth.

It wasn't the cheating; it was the lying, the betrayal, that made it impossible for me to stay with him. Had he come clean and been candid and open about his feelings, had we been able to talk it out and get to the heart of why he did what he did, I would have said, "Okay, let me see what we can do to work this out." I would have been willing to do that. Nobody's perfect and we all make mistakes and we all have demons that we have to deal with.

That Jimmy could not admit what he did—that he could not say he did it and apologize—was the determining factor for me. That meant that he would do it again. He could not be trusted.

We used to stay up all night and talk. We would talk about everything—our fantasies and the crazy thoughts we both had. I believed that there was nothing we couldn't talk about. But apparently there was. And I couldn't help but think, "What else was he hiding?" All he had to do was come clean. All he had to do was be honest with his feelings and I would have said, "Okay, let me see what we can do to work this out." I would have been willing to do that.

Jimmy was holding on to the lies. He never wanted to admit anything and he didn't want to get help. Had he even done that, I might have stayed. But because he kept running from the truth, I knew the situation would not change. I had to change. I had to start moving forward. I had to make some plans.

I am grateful every day that I didn't stay. And that even though it was a huge struggle financially, emotionally, and even physically to be without Jimmy, because I was able to make a stand for myself, God gave me a second chance.

One of the first things I did was enroll in nursing school. I didn't complete my degree the way my parents had hoped. I was basically a housewife for so many years. The only jobs I held were odd jobs here and there and my work with the group home. But I never had a job where I made enough money to really support myself and my children. I never made what Jimmy made. I needed a career and I was always someone who wanted to help people and thought becoming a nurse would be perfect.

But I sort of got sidetracked on my way to nursing school. I met Loren.

Getting into a relationship was the farthest thing from my mind. There was a carnival in town and I had taken my group home kids to it. We were near the arcade games and I noticed a man across the way looking at me. Maybe he noticed me looking at him. But almost like in a fairy tale, our eyes locked and there were instant sparks.

He walked over to talk to me. The teens that were with me had already gone to play an arcade game and I was standing there alone. He talked for a few minutes and somehow the subject of birthdays came up. I told him when my birthday was and he said, "So is mine!" I didn't believe him. He pulled out his wallet and sure enough we were born on the same day.

That was not enough, however, to start a relationship. In fact, I wasn't even thinking about him that way. But I gave him my number, and for some strange reason, I told him where I lived and we went our separate ways. I was excited and nervous and had butterflies in my stomach, and that was nice to feel after all those years. I hadn't felt that way for a very long time. I gathered my kids up and went back to the group home and dropped them off.

I went to pick up Brandon and Ebony from my sister-in-law's house. I told her about this nice man that I met earlier and how much we had in common, and we laughed about it in her kitchen over cake and coffee. After staying there for a while, Ebony, Brandon, and I headed home. When I got to our house, I noticed a car parked in front. When I got to the door, a man got out of the car and headed up the walkway. It was Loren. I was a little scared so I told Brandon and Ebony to go in the house and get ready for bed.

I couldn't believe he was at my door. And in the midst of being scared, I was also very flattered. He said he couldn't get me off his mind and had to see me and couldn't wait. It was bold of him and also very sincere. We talked on my front porch for a few minutes and decided to make a date for the next night to get to know one another better.

He left and I went inside to check on the kids. I felt like a schoolgirl all over again. And I was excited about going on a date. Loren swept me off my feet. He was so up front, so real. There were no pretenses about him. He answered all of my questions without hesitation and he made me feel completely comfortable around him.

After six weeks of dating, he asked me to marry him. "I know what I want and it's you and we can spend the next three years courting, but what's the point?" he said.

We were very attracted to each other. But I knew I couldn't go any further with him without a real commitment. I told him point blank. I had had enough of people playing with my life. Jimmy was the ultimate. I told him that I don't want to play any games. He said, "I don't want to play any games, I want to marry you."

I thought for a moment and said okay. Saying yes to marriage to a man that I had only known a few weeks was risky, but I looked at the fact that I had known Jimmy for almost three years before we married and it didn't make a difference. Knowing him three years didn't spare me any heartache when it came.

Of course, I was afraid that it might not work out. We were both afraid. But the night we decided to marry, Loren and I promised each other that we would not divorce. We promised that we would work out whatever adverse situations came our way. We had both been down an ugly road and neither of us ever wanted to journey there again.

He didn't propose on bended knee. There was no ring, no flowers, no dinner. It was a sober discussion between two adults. I made a decision that I thought would be beneficial not only to me but also to my children. I wasn't just living for myself. And this decision wasn't made on some whim from some schoolgirl excitement. I made a heady decision. Loren was a steady, stable man who could take care of us. He loved me and my children. But it wasn't enough that he loved us. And it wasn't enough that I loved him.

I had two children who had to come first. They had to be comfortable with him, too. Ebony was almost nine and Brandon was almost four. I knew they loved and respected me. And I believed that they would trust me enough to make good decisions for our life. I was very careful about dating and bringing men around them. But I was falling in love with Loren. Thank God, he won them over, too.

The only issue we had was what they were going to call him. Actually, that was Ebony's question to me. She already had a daddy, whom she loved and whom no one could replace (and I didn't want to replace him). Loren would be their stepfather, who would be living with us.

Loren had a nickname, which was strange for us. We didn't really do nicknames in our family except for "Junior" and "Baby Gail." Loren's nickname was "Snipper." I talked to him about how he would feel about the kids calling him Snipper. Would that be respectful?

We agreed that it was and it was a term of endearment. He didn't mind at all. Since I only called him "Loren," "Snipper" would distinguish the two relationships of him being my husband and being their stepfather. Ebony, Brandon, and my nieces and nephews call him Snipper to this day.

Our wedding didn't go through without a hitch.

After clearing it with my kids, I had to talk to my family. And one of my brothers reminded me of everything I had on my plate. There was nursing school on the horizon.

"You can't start too many new things at one time," my brother said. "Pick one, don't stress yourself out." He said I had to either decide to get married or decide to start a new career.

I decided on marriage. I figured I could go to school anytime.

I didn't want to just be dating a bunch of men or even one man just because I could. I wasn't that type of woman and I never wanted my children to see different men around. All of that "uncle this" and "uncle that" business that women thrust on their kids, I could not do. The dating game was a dead-end thing. I didn't like going out to clubs. I liked being home. I didn't want anyone calling me and asking me for dates. I didn't like that.

Loren was becoming a fixture in our home in a short time and I didn't want there to be any confusion. He was either here to stay or he had to go.

I decided to keep him.

My decision could have easily backfired on me. I'm not saying that it almost didn't and I'm not saying that my marriage is perfect. But it's been more than twenty years going now and we're not finished yet.

After he asked me to marry him, we took a drive out to the beach, a very nice man-made beach. We were outside holding hands, walking along the water.

It was a very romantic evening. While out there I was overwhelmed with a feeling of déjà vu. I had dreamed of that very scene, holding hands with a man who looked just like Loren.

I dreamed about him before I ever met him. I dreamed about holding hands with a man with salt-and-pepper hair. I couldn't see his features; it was a silhouette of a man but it felt like Loren. This man was tall like Loren and had the same complexion and hair as Loren. Perhaps that's why he felt so familiar to me that day at the carnival. I had seen him before in my dreams.

Loren was also divorced with two children—a boy and a girl—just like me. We liked a lot of the same things. We were both homebodies who didn't like a lot of drama. Our decision to get married was not as whimsical as it was practical. We had an agreement. It was real, not based on a big elaborate wedding and a two-carat diamond ring.

We got married at the church that Jimmy and I attended. We got married after a Sunday service. We had the same minister—the one who told me to go back home and be a better wife to Jimmy. That's the church that my kids and I still attended and he was still the minister, so we rolled with that.

It was a beautiful church and we had a very small ceremony. I made sure that my best friend, Roxanne (who is now deceased), was there. Whatever family that was in town attended. Loren's parents weren't there. His father was an invalid and his mother was deceased. We could have gone down to the court-house. But I wanted us to stand before God and say our vows.

We said our "I do's" and Loren even put the ring on the correct finger. Even the kiss was perfect. I still think about that kiss to this day. It was absolutely perfect.

We didn't have a honeymoon. We both had to work. He moved into the house that I lived in. We ended up moving into our own home together a little later, but everything went smoothly. We settled into our life as if we had been married for years.

The summer we got married was exciting. My children were away with Jimmy, and Loren was in a color guard marching group and I would follow him to all of the parades all over Ohio. It was so much fun. To this day we enjoy going to parades and festivals. It's part of our life.

One of the reasons why I knew Loren was the "right" man was because of how smooth a transition it was and how comfortable we all were with him. I never believed I would ever be able to love another man after Jimmy. I just couldn't see it.

Loren was my first relationship with a promise for a future. Right before I met Loren, I had sworn off all men. I had put them all in one category—dogs. I had dated a couple of guys in between Jimmy and Loren. They all had the same thing on their mind—to get me in bed. And when I told them about Jimmy—who was completely out of the picture and whom I barely spoke to at this point—and his hidden lifestyle, they all made jokes about it, which I didn't appreciate. They didn't seem to get it.

While I hated dating, I couldn't quite settle into the idea of being single either. I dated because I felt I should. I was still a young woman and I didn't want to just sit around the house waiting to get old, but my heart wasn't in it until I met Loren.

There was an instant connection. And when I told him about my life with Jimmy, he took me seriously. Loren seemed to understand what it had done to me. He also understood how important my children's well-being was to me, how important a family was to me. He connected.

And the connection was made stronger when Ebony and Brandon took to him almost immediately. When they came back from Jimmy's at the end of the summer, we settled into a family instantly. I was worried about how that would work—this new man living in our home. We worked out what to call him, but we didn't discuss with them how this thing was going to work.

There was also the issue of disciplining the children. I didn't want to ever hear, "You aren't my father!" from my children when it came to Loren. We decided that we would both discipline them but I would take the lead. And that seemed to work out well.

The kids didn't rebel. But Jimmy did. I didn't tell

him about Loren, someone else did, and he hit the roof. He didn't like it one bit. He gave me such a hard time.

Within the year, I was pregnant. And when Jimmy found out I was pregnant, he took me to court to get dual custody of our children. He already got his visitation rights—which was every other weekend and the summers. But he wanted more. Actually, I don't believe he wanted more. I believe he just wanted to hurt me.

One of the summers when the kids were supposed to stay with him, he took them to his mother's. Ebony was not happy, so she called and said she wanted to come home. She said she was sick. I dropped everything and was practically at Jimmy's mother's house before Ebony hung up the phone. I took my kids back home. Jimmy used that against me in court, saying I violated our agreement. The judge found me in contempt and fined me.

Jimmy tried to create a lot of drama because I had dared to remarry. I was still his wife in his eyes. Loren was wonderful during this period. He didn't escalate the situation or add fuel to the fire. In fact, he handled it wonderfully and even tried to smooth things over with Jimmy. And because we didn't feed into the negativity, we were blessed.

We gave birth to a beautiful baby boy, Loren III. For Loren, who had an older daughter who lived with her mother in another city and a grown son who lived in another state, this child was his pride and joy.

And for me, it just made our family that much closer. Loren III became the thread that tied us all together into one big family.

There was an initial concern that there would be jealousy, but that all disappeared when Loren III was brought home. Ebony and Brandon helped spoil their little brother and watched over him more than we could have imagined. He is still spoiled by them to this day.

Jimmy eventually came around. He had no choice. Loren wasn't going anywhere and neither was our bond. He not only grew to accept Loren, but Loren III even spent time during the summers with Jimmy when Brandon and Ebony went to visit. For years Loren III would cry when his brother and sister would leave for Jimmy's. He wanted to go. We asked Jimmy if it was okay for him to come, too. He agreed. And by the end of their visit he ended up accepting Loren III as his own, too.

It took us a long time to heal. It took a lot of prayer and a lot of faith. But today we are truly one big happy family with a lot of love and a whole lot of understanding.

Chapter 4

COVER GIRL

Men who are living on the down low need an accomplice—a woman. They don't want the world to think that they are gay, so you will never see a down low man without a woman in his life. She is his cover. She provides him with the shield to protect him from prying eyes and whispers within the community. Because a down low man doesn't view himself as a homosexual—at least he will deny publicly that he is gay—he must have a cover girl.

Most women who are married to or dating a DL man have no idea that their man is on the down low. And there are many women who will never know. But there are certain "types" of women that a DL man is attracted to and will pursue.

While no woman can be put in a box because we are all different, there are three basic personality types that are particularly attractive to men on the DL or men who are living a lie and need a cover.

Bishop T.D. Jakes deals with this subject in his novel, *Cover Girls*. In the opening chapter there is an exchange between Tonya and Michelle that can be applied to the way a lot of women view their roles in relationships and what they are willing to do to get or keep a man. Michelle takes Tonya to task for not looking out for herself: "Cinderella was a lie! . . . I mean, if you keep cleaning up other people's messes, if you keep inviting other people to dinner and allowing them to eat first, you are not going to get the prince . . . What you're going to get, sister girl, is leftovers."

Women are notorious for putting others first and not taking care of themselves. The Lord helps those who help themselves. You cannot lift someone else up unless you are first on steady ground. And the need to nurture and want to be there for your mate is natural—but not if it means you diminish yourself in the process.

While I have outlined three basic categories that a cover girl will fall under, they all have something in common—they are willing to put the needs of their men (and other people in their lives) before their needs. They are willing to let everyone else eat first.

That was me. But I have learned over the years if Brenda doesn't eat first, she will starve waiting for someone to feed her. I have learned to take care of my needs and make sure that I am being respected and not allow anyone to walk all over me. But getting here took a very long time and a whole lot of pain and hurt that I had to get through.

As a new bride, I let a lot of things my husband did and said slide by. I didn't want to make trouble. But every hurtful remark and action was a sign of things to come. And every time I let him get away with it opened the door for him to take things one step further.

Type 1: Wide-Eyed and Just Plain Naive

This is the category that I fit into. A DL man loves a woman who is not worldly and who will completely dote and depend on him. This is a perfect woman for a DL man. And in many ways, I was the perfect wife/cover girl for Jimmy.

Our marriage was storybook. We were both virgins and our wedding night was memorable. He was attentive, sensitive, and wonderful—not that I had anything to compare it to. But he seemed to do everything right.

But looking back, almost from the beginning things were not right. Jimmy was very controlling and I let him control me. Jimmy was my everything, so I did whatever he told me to do.

He would tell me what to wear to church, how to speak, whom to like. I allowed him to control my friendships. You don't upset the household. You don't go against his authority. I'm sure he could see that he could control me. Then he could live his life the way he wanted to.

I allowed him to control my whole life. I was naive, I was shy, and I thought the world of him. Everything he said was law. I trusted him. That's the way I was raised. Once a man becomes your husband, he's the head of the household, and you do things to please him. You don't upset the household. You don't go against his authority. I'm sure he could see when he met me that he could control me. I am certain, even if it were subconscious, he wanted to marry me because I was so naive and because I was so wide-eyed and easily led, allowing him to live his life the way he wanted to.

Men who are on the down low look for women they can fool—these men feel they can pull the wool over the eyes of such women. They want young girls, sheltered women who won't ask many questions and who won't hassle them. This isn't unique to men on the down low, nor is it unique in the United States of America.

During a six-day International AIDS Conference in Thailand in 2004, Population Services International announced that in sub-Saharan Africa the largest-growing group of newly infected HIV cases were girls ages fourteen to twenty whose lovers were married, middle-aged men. A teenage girl in southern Africa is five times more likely to be HIV-infected than a teen-age boy.

The article said: "These older men don't wear condoms and prefer the younger women partly on the be-lief that they'll be 'pure' but also to gain 'status' among friends, according to surveys of both men and teenage girls in Kenya, Uganda and South Africa."

Mercy Amba Oduyoye, director of the Institute of Women, Religion, and Culture in Ghana, said the problem stems from societies dominated by males, and that the girls are coerced. "Defiling a minor can hardly be consensual," she said.

And for a man who needs a cover, what better wife or girlfriend than someone who is easily manipu-lated? It's much easier for an older man to take advan-tage of a younger woman. It's easier to impress a younger woman. It's easier to get away with things when dealing with a young woman who hasn't lived much. It's a control thing. To this day, Jimmy still tries to control me, but I am not that same young girl I was when I met him. And there's not much that he can get away with.

Type 2: Women Who Are Running Low— Low on Self-Esteem and Self-Image

I fit this category as well. At least I was beaten into this category. After the storybook wedding, we moved to Turkey where Jimmy was stationed. I got pregnant shortly after we married and had a baby girl, Ebony, there.

Little by little, Jimmy started changing. He started making little comments about me that were belittling, and he put me in positions that made me uncomfortable and even made me feel bad about myself. I never shared this with anyone because I always felt that it was my fault. That's what happens a lot of time with women—and because they feel it's their fault, they don't speak out. When Jimmy was acting out or feeling like he wanted to do something to violate the relationship, he would turn it around and make me feel bad. He would start a fight with me that I believed was somehow my fault.

When we were in Turkey, Jimmy's friend Paul practically lived with us. He would come over every day for dinner and would often stay long after I had turned in for the night. He made himself really comfortable. It was not unusual for Paul to come over from the base and say, "Sis, what's for dinner?" He would even ask me to make him certain meals. He started acting like he was the man of our home. And being the dutiful wife who didn't want to make waves and who wanted to keep the peace, I would acquiesce and fix Paul dinner. But I resented Jimmy for allowing this man to come in and tell me what to do.

I was very cordial. I kept to myself that I really didn't like him. Jimmy didn't like it when I told him that I didn't care for his friends, so I didn't share how I was feeling. I finally pulled Jimmy aside one evening and said, "Don't you think Paul needs to go home?" He told me off and made me feel so bad that I never said anything again. I was turning into a doormat.

One day I had baked a carrot cake. I had gotten a recipe from a lady and I wanted to perfect it. I was trying to make it taste like the cake baked by the lady who gave me the recipe. I had been working on it for a few weeks. And it was perfect. I was so proud of it.

I had put on a little weight after having the baby and Jimmy had started making little comments. He came home and I said, "Look at the carrot cake I made. It's perfect." And he said, "We don't need more cake! You're getting fat." And we got into a heated discussion about the cake and he said, "I'll throw it out!" And I said, "Throw it out, then!" And he did. I was very upset about it. But I thought about it and convinced myself that he was right. He was only looking out for me, I would tell myself.

But that wasn't the truth. Women will lie to themselves and let their men get away with things rather than stand up for themselves and face the facts. And I'm not saying that every man who belittles his wife or girlfriend is on the down low; I'm saying that women who allow men to be verbally abusive or even mentally and physically abusive must take a long look at themselves. Because if you allow someone to abuse you, you do not love yourself. And if you don't love yourself, you leave the door open for someone to mistreat you.

DL men are very attracted to women who don't love themselves. For me, I was lured in with a perfect picture that turned fuzzy, and I stayed because I hoped that it would return to perfect and because there were still enough perfect moments to hold out hope. But the reality was, I was scared and I didn't love myself enough to confront the truth—I wasn't being treated right. And I wasn't confident enough to demand better treatment. So I took it, mostly in silence. And I stayed.

You will see a lot of DL men with women who are very overweight. If a woman is struggling with obesity, she has some self-esteem issues. You can't possibly love yourself if you are eating yourself to death. That fat is a symptom of a greater ill, and men on the prowl prey on that.

A woman approached me after a speaking engagement in Springfield, Ohio. She told me that she found out that her husband was on the DL. She said that she was the perfect wife and couldn't understand what she needed to do to keep him. She didn't want a divorce; she loved him. As I asked her more questions, I found out that her desire to keep her husband had more to do with her belief that she couldn't find another man, and the fact that her husband wanted to be with her, despite how fat she was, meant that he must really love her. She was about five-feet-five and weighed about three hundred pounds. She had a very pretty face but I could tell that she didn't feel good about herself.

She, like most women, couldn't see herself without a man. She needed to have a man. A lot of women believe that they are nothing without a man. But the truth is they really believe they are nothing even *with* the man. These women need to focus on loving who they are—even at three hundred pounds. And that if they are letting anyone degrade them, they are allowing that person to kill their spirit—the perfect spirit that God gave them.

You are God's creation; therefore, the goal is to believe that and know that. And once you embrace and love who you are, then you won't allow someone to disrespect you or take advantage of you. And what's funny is that people somehow know this and don't even try.

When I started standing up for myself, Jimmy was shocked. And it changed our relationship. Even after the divorce, we were able to eventually become friends again because I drew a line that he knew he couldn't cross. I defined clearly for him who I really was and what I was not willing to put up with.

Type 3: She's on the DL, Too!

A few women who are with men on the DL have something to hide, too. Maybe they have a drug habit or perhaps they are a lesbian. Or maybe they're a gold digger, looking for a sugar daddy. Whatever the case, there are women who marry men that they know or suspect of being on the DL because they want to get something out of the situation or they are looking for a cover, too.

In Hollywood there are rumors of couples who are

married to one another to cover for one another. This, to me, is the most honest of all of these relationships. If a woman and a man get together with each of them knowing exactly what the other is all about—even if they are both hiding it from the world—that's fine. That's their business.

Unfortunately, the majority of the women who are in relationships with men on the DL have no idea. And even if that little voice inside of them is working overtime, the men know that these women are too insecure or too desperate ever to question them. That's manipulative and it's costing lives.

Women have to wake up. They have to first love themselves and work on building up themselves and not define their self-worth or value on the man they have or don't have. If women put their energy into finding themselves instead of finding a man, perhaps there would be less horror stories like mine. I know if I'd waited, as my parents had wanted me to, and gone to school and finished my degree, I would have had enough life experience to be able to discern things about Jimmy that seem so obvious to me today.

But I believe that everything happens for a reason. And my experience living and loving Jimmy King for all of those years taught me a lot about life and loving myself. It also put me in a position to help other women. I want to take the cover off the Cover Girls and empower women to not be victimized by men on the DL.

If a man can smell your nectar, whether it is sweet or sour, he will act accordingly. So how you feel about yourself and what you project to the world will determine in many ways how you will be treated.

Let's dissect the term *self-esteem*. For a long time I didn't know what low self-esteem really meant. And I didn't know that I had it. I know there are many women who have low self-esteem and have been knocked down and trodden on by others and even trampled on by their own actions and may not recognize it. There are some symptoms, however, that can be a tip-off that someone may be suffering from low self-esteem, which I look at as an illness like cancer or diabetes. It is a sickness that has cost many lives. Women with low self-esteem allow things to happen to them that should not, and sometimes it not only means a bad relationship or two; it can mean their very life.

Do you look in the mirror and check yourself frequently and find the following:

Too fat
Too skinny
Legs too small
Legs too big
Hips too wide
Hips too narrow
Skin too dark
Skin too light
Too tall

Too short
Lips too big
Lips too thin
Hair too short
Hair too kinky

If you find that there are too many things "wrong" with you when you look in the mirror, you may suffer from low self-esteem. It is natural to see your flaws, but how do you react to the things you see? Today when I look in the mirror, there may be things that I would like to change, like losing a pound or two, but I love every inch of my being. I love myself—with my flaws—because I know that although I am not perfect in the physical realm, I am God's child and that makes me perfect in a much more important place.

Do people tell you that you are not intelligent, or do you tell yourself that you are not intelligent?

Are you never pleased with how something turns out that you put together? Do you criticize yourself or internalize the criticism from others? Do you wish you were someone else? If you answer yes to any of these questions, you have low self-esteem. Instead of focusing on the negative things, spend an hour each morning before you even talk to another human being reminding yourself how special you are. Find five wonderful things about you and tell yourself how wonderful you are. Start your day off right—focusing on what's right about you.

God made you fearfully and wonderfully. God

loves you just the way you are. Unless your weight is a health issue, you need to accept yourself the way you are and love yourself more. Once you love yourself, you open up the door for others to sense that and love you, too.

I have learned if someone has only negative things to say about me, that person doesn't deserve to be in my life. If a person makes me feel bad about myself, that person doesn't deserve to be in my life. I have to love myself enough to get rid of negativity and negative people.

One of my favorite songs is "Wildflower" by New Birth, which describes a woman as a "gentle flower growin' wild."

I see people as wildflowers—beautiful when left alone to grow, when they are not cultivated and shaped to become something they are not, something others want them to be. Wildflowers come in all shapes, sizes, and colors—just as God has made us in all shapes, sizes, and colors. And just like wildflowers, no matter our shape, size, or color, we are all beautiful.

Chapter 5

THE SIGNS

In *On the Down Low,* Jimmy suggests that there are no real signs to know if your man is on the DL. Jimmy and I have had several conversations about this since his book came out in 2004, and he doesn't believe that there are definitive signs. According to him, a man who likes to decorate and likes to bake cookies is not necessarily on the down low. And just because a man likes football and is "hard" doesn't mean that he's not.

While I agree that there is no way of telling if a man is gay or on the DL just by his interests or even the way he carries himself, I do believe in what is called "gaydar." I do believe that people who are living a double life throw off a certain kind of energy. And as a follower of the Word, I do know there is such a thing as discernment.

But since leaving Jimmy and thinking back, I had a feeling about every one of Jimmy's friends whom he tried to push on me as "good people." And because of my experience with these men and with Jimmy, I can spot a DL man or a gay man on contact. I can see it in their eyes. I can tell by their mannerisms.

Oh, it's not blatant, but I can tell now. It's part of my intuition. I'm not paranoid. I just have a sixth sense. I trust my intuition. I don't confront people when I have these inklings. I am just cautious. And I have learned if you get bad vibes or strange vibes around someone and you have to constantly justify a person's behavior or attitudes in order for you to feel good about them being in your life, you are probably better off without them in your life.

Of course, you do this after looking in the mirror and checking yourself.

I believe all women possess a sixth sense about things, and when it comes to our men, we don't necessarily listen to that little voice inside. But we must put that sixth sense in overdrive because it will tell you exactly what you need to know. Looking back, there were several signs there for me that I chose to ignore.

When I first got married, I was so in love and so naive that Jimmy was able to get away with a lot of things that should have sent gongs off in my head. But I didn't want to see the signs. Many women would rather ignore what they're feeling or seeing because they want to keep their relationship and they don't want to rock the boat.

Below are some signs that were there for me that should have signaled trouble. But I ignored them.

1. He's never accountable with his time.

Jimmy would say, "I'll be back," and later I would find out that he claimed to be at work and wasn't. I never followed him or hovered over him. I wasn't possessive of his time and I wasn't up on his every move. I believed what he told me. When I worked, I worked a second shift and I found out that he would leave the house shortly after I did, after getting a babysitter, and he would return home before I ever knew that he was ever gone. So he had time to do anything he wanted—and he did.

When we moved to San Antonio, Jimmy and I would entertain a lot, having cookouts and card parties. Paul and his wife were regular fixtures at our house. She and I were card partners. And it never failed, as soon as she and I would sit down to play, Jimmy and Paul would find a way to sneak off somewhere.

"Babe, we're going to get some beer," Jimmy would say. And he and Paul would be off. Thinking back, I don't remember if he came back with the beer or not. I do know they would be gone a long time. I never thought anything about it because I wasn't suspicious. I believed that Jimmy was going to get beer.

One time we went camping with two other couples, including Paul and his wife. When the men went off to fish, the women stayed behind and tended the camp while the children played. I do remember the men coming back with very few fish for us to cook. Thinking back on it now, I wonder if fishing was all they were doing. I wonder about a lot of things Jimmy did back then. I wonder about the times he said he was going out to get something from the store or the numerous times he said he had to work late. I didn't think about it then because I wasn't trained that way. He picked the perfect wife—someone who wouldn't hassle him or question him. I patterned my life after June Cleaver. I was the classic Stepford Wife. My husband ruled the house. He was the head of the household and I didn't question much at all. I trusted him and I never questioned where he went or why. I learned later what a huge mistake that was on my part. It allowed him to get away with so much.

2. His behavior is inconsistent.

I would get undivided attention and then two weeks later Jimmy acted like he didn't want to be around me (see Chapter 6, "Identity Crisis: Dr. Jekyll/Mr. Hyde"). He would run hot and cold. He would be sweet as pie one week and then real nasty the next. He would bring flowers and candy, and the next day he would be grumbling about something I did and treating me like dirt.

He was the quintessential Dr. Jekyll/Mr. Hyde, and

I have grown to learn that this split personality was directly connected to his covert activities outside of our marriage. When he was feeling like he needed to explore something or someone, he would get antsy and pick a fight so he could have an excuse to leave.

Jimmy had it good. I wasn't the detective (at first) that many women are. I trusted him, so he was able to do a lot of things many men would have had difficulties doing. And because our work schedules were so different, he could do so without me ever knowing.

3. His friends are a little too friendly.

When I first met Jimmy, he didn't have a whole lot of friends. He didn't hang out with a bunch of boys, and I liked that about him. He was able to become so close to my family because my brothers and sisters became like his family, too.

It wasn't until we moved to Turkey that I started to raise an eyebrow. He got involved with this military club called Occasions Anonymous. It was primarily men in their thirties and forties, and we were in our early twenties. I never felt comfortable the few times Jimmy would bring me to club functions. I was content just being with Jimmy, especially after having Ebony. I liked the idea of the three of us being one happy family together. I loved the times we spent together being parents. But Jimmy seemed to want more.

It seemed like the men and women of Occasions

Anonymous not only were too old for us but also had nothing in common with us. But Jimmy insisted on us being a part of it. He seemed to enjoy being around those "old men." I didn't detest the old geezers, but they were the kind of men who would lick their lips and shake their Mr. T Gold Chain Kit when they saw a young woman come in the room. And they would undress you with their eyes.

I also didn't like that they drank too much. It made me uncomfortable. Not that I was holier that thou, but the alcohol seemed to make people too loud and ignorant. But there was more. When one wife of a serviceman in Jimmy's unit who befriended me found out that Jimmy had joined the club, she took me to the side and said, "Don't you know that that club swaps wives?"

I immediately told Jimmy that he had to turn in his membership. I drew the line. And he did. But he seemed to go from one bad thing to another.

One evening Jimmy came home from the base and told me, "I met somebody that I want you to meet. He's cool people and he happens to have the same last name as your maiden name. Isn't that something?"

"That *is* cool!" I said, intrigued. "Maybe he's a relative."

Jimmy brought Paul home the next night. And immediately, I didn't like him. I couldn't put my finger on it. Maybe it was that he was too familiar, too quick. He just sort of came in and made himself at home. He started calling me sis just after a couple of days of knowing me and would come over and never know when to leave.

As their friendship progressed and Paul was always around, it became more uncomfortable for me. It wasn't anything Paul was doing. It was his way, his tone. He started bossing me around like I was *his* wife. And what infuriated me was that Jimmy would let him. It was like I had two husbands.

After working on the base, they would come in the house. Paul acted like he lived there. The familiarity and family-like atmosphere were the norm for military families because they were all away from home. So it wasn't unusual to have someone so close from the base. But Paul would take it too far. One night he came in and said, "Why haven't you cooked yet? And what's for dinner?" He was dead serious.

I was very cordial. I kept to myself that I really didn't like him. Jimmy didn't like it when I told him that I didn't care for his friends, so I didn't share how I was feeling. I went in the kitchen and I cooked some meat loaf and gravy, mashed potatoes, and some carrots. He enjoyed it. The next night it was the same thing: "What's for dinner?" That night I made lahana, which is cabbage leaves, tomatoes, and rice cooked in olive oil. It was one of the traditional Turkish dishes that I learned to make and I'd perfected it. He seemed to enjoy that, too. But I wasn't enjoying his company at all.

When Jimmy was around Paul, it was Paul who became the man of the house. Jimmy seemed to follow up on everything Paul did and seemed to listen to everything Paul said. Paul had a maid in Turkey in his apartment, so Jimmy had to get a maid. Since I wasn't working and I kept a very nice home, I didn't think we needed a maid. But Paul said we needed a maid because it looked good for a brother to have a maid. So we got a maid. Come to find out, Paul's maid was doing more than cleaning his apartment.

And when it was time for us to move from Turkey and back to the States, Jimmy told me we had two choices—San Antonio, Texas, or Washington, D.C. I wanted to go to D.C. because I had heard it was a progressive city, our nation's capital, and it was closer to our home in Ohio. But I really didn't have a choice. Jimmy wanted to go to San Antonio. Why? Because that's where Paul lived. Jimmy said we were going to San Antonio because, "Washington is too expensive."

"I don't want to go to San Antonio," I told him.

"Well, there are no choices!" he said. "We have to go to San Antonio."

"There are no other choices?!"

"No!"

He brought the papers home saying we were going to San Antonio. And I yelled, "I told you I don't want to go to San Antonio!"

"Well, this is where we're going," he said. "It's a done deal."

End of argument, we were going to San Antonio.

He convinced me I would meet Paul's wife and that we had a lot in common. Paul was convincing Jimmy to go to San Antonio. He was telling him, "Your family could be with my family and we can all be together." And Jimmy bought it. I don't know why Paul's wife and child weren't in Turkey with him. I never asked. Thinking back on it, though, it was very strange for him to be in Turkey with a wife and child back in the States. I guess that's the way Paul wanted it.

Paul was what could be considered fine at that time. He was about six feet tall with a nice build, light skin, light eyes, and curly hair. He had keen features. But he was ugly to me—overbearing, controlling my husband and my household. He was a pest and now we were moving to the same town to live near him. I was miserable. But like a "good" wife, I didn't say much. I put on a good face and we moved.

Once we got to San Antonio, it was even worse than in Turkey. Paul and Jimmy spent all of their time together. Jimmy would rather hang out with Paul than spend time with me. I found out after reading *On the Down Low* how close he and Paul really were. But if I had been watching more closely during that period, I would not have needed the book to find out.

You have to pay attention to men who spend that much time together and who would rather be with each other than their wives or girlfriends. Something is going on.

Jimmy had quite a few friends who I didn't care for

and who raised my eyebrows. But when I questioned Jimmy about these men, he would always say the same thing. "You have to get to know him," Jimmy would say. "He's good people."

We stayed in San Antonio three years before Jimmy was discharged from the military, and then we headed back home to Ohio. Some man named Melvin called at the house after we moved back there. He sounded a little funny to me on the phone, like a punk—which is what we called homosexuals back then.

"Jimmy, who is Thomas?" I asked.

"Oh, he's good people," Jimmy said. "You should meet him."

Good people? Here we go with that.

Jimmy felt that if he could get me to know them, then it would be okay to have these people around. His friends became my friends. He forced them on me—their wives, their children. I ended up very close to Paul's wife. I liked her a lot. She was a beautiful person. But I never really had any friends that I made on my own because Jimmy wouldn't really let me have friends outside of his circle. But his friends were always welcome.

There was another sign in this. Men who are living a double life are usually more jealous and extra protective of their women. Either they are suspicious because they know what they are doing, or they want to make sure they control their woman so that they can continue to do their dirt and she will have no place to turn.

So be careful of a man who is too close to his friends and at the same time doesn't want you to have any friends.

4. The sex changes.

Toward the end of our relationship, another thing that tipped me off that something was seriously wrong was the difference in our sex life. Jimmy used to be very attentive and very amorous. He was the one who initiated sex most of the time. But the times that he wanted it decreased from every day to once a week or once every other week.

It was a noticeable change. I even asked him, "Why aren't we being intimate?" As usual, I thought it was me. Things didn't feel right. Months would pass and we hadn't had sex, and I thought I had done something wrong. He never gave me an answer.

When we would have sex, it was like going through the motions. We were practically platonic friends, raising two children and living in the same house. I started to feel really bad about myself and I didn't know what to do. It was actually a relief to find out that he was cheating because it explained a lot.

Before his relationship with Melvin, there were a few clues as well. It was shortly after we lost our twins. Jimmy was very supportive during this period, which was tough on both of us. We were healing and heading to a nice place in our relationship. One evening while we were being intimate, he made an unusual request. Actually he didn't ask; he positioned me the way he wanted me and began to penetrate me. After a few tries, I had to say something.

"This is not right," I said. "This is uncomfortable and I don't like it."

"You'll get used to it," he said.

"No, I won't get used to it."

"You never know until you try it," he said.

So I let him try it. But before he could get into it, I stopped him.

"You have to stop," I said. "This is too uncomfortable."

That was the first and only time Jimmy tried to have anal sex with me. But that one time produced a flood of questions in my mind.

Why did he want to try that? Where did he learn that? And why did he think I would get used to it?

Looking back now, that should have been my smoking gun. I'm not saying that men who like anal sex are homosexual or on the down low. In normal relationships couples experiment and it is within the boundaries of a relationship to try new and different things. But for us, it was highly out of the norm.

When we got married, I was a virgin and Jimmy said he was, too. When I think back, Jimmy probably was a virgin at the time—a virgin when it came to women. When he wrote in his book that he knew of his attraction to men since he was eight, it makes me wonder if he had ever acted on it before he was sexual with me. It makes me wonder exactly when he had his very first sexual experience.

Either he had a great imagination or he had some experience. The thing I loved most about Jimmy was that he liked to talk. We talked a lot about things, including our sexual fantasies. He never once mentioned even having a fantasy about anal sex. But on this particular night he just turns me over and tries it—no warning. And it seemed like he knew exactly what he was doing.

So I questioned in my mind where he'd learned it because he didn't learn it from me. If we were going to do something like that, I would have preferred to be in on it from the beginning. It's something we should have explored together, not something that was thrust on me the way it was. After the Melvin discovery, I replayed that scene over in my head, and I know that it was a clear sign that I should have paid attention to.

5. He hides his pornography.

I kept a spotless house. I hate clutter and dirt. Yes, I am a neat freak. When I was married to Jimmy, I was fanatical about keeping the house clean and would make the rounds in the house from cleaning the windows to dusting every corner. On this particular day I was cleaning the closets. I entered our walk-in closet and almost walked out when I noticed Jimmy's side of the closet in disarray. I figured he must have been in a real hurry that morning. I hung up the clothes Jimmy had thrown on the floor.

One of the items was an oversized green peacoat—a military coat that he never wore. It took up so much room in the closet that I decided to pack it up to give to the Salvation Army. He had no use for a heavy peacoat in sunny, hot San Antonio.

So I went through the pockets to make sure there was no money or anything of value left in the coat. Stuck in one of the pockets was a magazine.

"Why does Jimmy have magazines stuck in his pocket?" I thought. "What are these magazines, *Playboy*? He doesn't have to hide his girly magazines from me."

We talked about everything, and he knew I would have no problem with him having girly magazines. We had such a close and open relationship that I could see no reason for him to hide anything from me. When our heads hit the pillows each night, no matter how tired we were, or what had transpired over the course of a day, we could open up to each other and discuss anything; practically all night.

I was hurt that he was hiding something from me. But when I opened the magazine, I understood why it was hidden in the closet, rolled up in a coat he never wore. It wasn't a *Playboy* magazine but something called *Blue Boy Blues*. The magazine was full of naked men in all kinds of suggestive poses.

"Why does he want these?" I thought. *Duh!*

Believe it or not, I never asked. I just brushed it all aside, folded the magazine back up, and put it back in the pocket just as I'd found it. Maybe I felt by ignoring what I found, it would go away. If Jimmy wanted to think that he could hide something in a house that I cleaned from top to bottom, fine. It was his secret, as far as I was concerned. I just shook my head in wonderment of why he would have such things, and in hiding. I went about cleaning the rest of the closet, my side. I really didn't want to find anything else that was not meant for my eyes. And I never mentioned the magazine to him—not until I confronted him later about Melvin.

I was extremely naive, and I ignored or brushed over things that should have sent me running or at the very least into a confrontation with Jimmy. I didn't want to make waves; I didn't want to rock our boat. Like a lot of women, I wanted peace at any cost. But that could have cost me my life. I have learned that I love myself enough not to let anyone ever take advantage of me again, nor will I allow things just to go past me without examining them.

At the same time, it is important not to live a paranoid life. Trust is an important element in any relationship, and once that trust is broken, it is time to move on. Broken trust is one of the hardest things to repair. If you have to keep following a grown man like a detective and sniffing around for clues and if you keep finding questionable things, perhaps that's not the man for you.

You have to pay attention to not only what that man does but also what he says. If he tells you, "I'm not good enough for you," believe it. Jimmy used to say that to me. I now know if someone says something like that, believe him . . . and move on.

I have discernment now and my spirit is able to discover the things I need to know. I don't live a paranoid life. I let my husband show me his merits, and I stepped out on faith that our relationship would work. And it has. Just because I had a previous relationship that was built on lies doesn't mean that I will forever make Loren pay for the sins of someone else. However, that's exactly what I was doing in the very beginning. I was doubting him and not trusting him.

I quickly realized that Loren should have the right to start with a clean slate. He should be innocent until proven guilty. He got a clean slate. But I wasn't a fool the second time around. I watched from the start and let him show me who he was. I went in with both eyes wide open. And he showed himself to be a man worthy of my trust.

Chapter 6

IDENTITY CRISIS:
DR. JEKYLL/MR. HYDE

People always ask, "How could you not know?" It seems so obvious to them that Jimmy, now J.L., was definitely on the DL. But I did not know. I had no idea, no clue. There were plenty of signs, looking back in hindsight. But that's hindsight. What I do know, and this may be true for a lot of men, is that Jimmy was a very good actor. In fact, he was a sort of personality chameleon. And looking back, I realize that his desire to be different people and change his personality should have been a real tip-off. But I simply didn't pay attention. He spent most of his time in our relationship being "perfect."

One of the first things I noticed about Jimmy was his unique style. That's one of the things that attracted me to him. Jimmy had a flare about him that could have easily led people to mistake him for a model. He had charisma and style, and was good-looking.

He was even voted best dressed in high school. There was a school dance in his senior year called "Class Night." We had just started going out and Jimmy invited me to be his date. He picked me up and that was the first time that I really noticed how sharp he was. Everything was pressed to a crisp, his shoes were shined to a high gloss, and he was well groomed. I was also impressed because he had a car—a clean car. Most boys in my school were still walking.

I must say that evening sealed the deal for me—I was hooked. (Yes, it was a little pretentious of me to judge him from the outside, but I was sixteen years old. And thankfully, I have since learned my lesson in that area.)

Jimmy was romantic—romantic in the ways you read about men being in romance novels. After we got married, Jimmy was immediately shipped off to Michigan for training. He would send me love letters and cards every week. I looked forward to the mailman coming. I would anticipate and sometimes even wait for him because I knew there would be something special for me.

I still have many of the letters, notes, and cards Jimmy sent me. These letters and cards were not just filled with "I love you's," although there were plenty of those. It was the way he expressed himself that could make me melt. He was poetic and just always knew the right things to say.

I don't know why I kept some of the letters and cards. During our marriage, I would often take out the box that I kept them in and reread some of them. It would rekindle the old sparks and remind me why I fell in love with him. After our divorce, I never looked at those letters and cards. They collected dust in that box until recently. I had been unable to read them because they were a reminder of how much of a fraud he was and how gullible I must have been.

I believe I kept them after our marriage was over not for some sentimental reason, but because I knew one day I would have to face the truth and those letters and cards would be part of my healing. And I was right. I sat down one Saturday afternoon alone in my house and went through those letters. I cried. I laughed. And I came to a few realizations that I was not able to come to before—Jimmy wasn't fooling me. He was fooling himself.

I also made another discovery—his letters began to change over the years. It wasn't just his tone, but even his signature. When the letters first started to come, he would sign them "James." I never called him James. No one in his family called him James. But I guess he felt more mature signing "James."

Then I noticed his signature started to change. He started signing "Jimi" with the *i*'s dotted with a big circle. I never asked him about it, but I think he felt that "Jimmy" was too common. So he started spelling his name the way Jimi Hendrix did. I had even tried to follow suit by spelling my name "Brinda" with an *i* for a short while. Imagine that.

He stayed Jimi for a short time. Then after our divorce

he started working as an AIDS activist. He then started talking about down low brothers and he became "J.L." I never asked him why he changed to J.L. but I figured it was to become somewhat anonymous. And then I noticed he would refer to himself as "Jay"—not to be confused with that J.L. guy who was talking about that DL stuff in Springfield, Ohio.

With each new name, there was a different personality. With each new name, there was a different man. Jimmy was the man that I had married. That Jimmy was "Mr. Right." He was the kind of young man that I could bring home to Mama. He knew all the right things to say; he was well mannered. He was proper and from the "right" family. Jimmy came from an upstanding family. His father was a deacon in the Baptist Church and his mother was a devoted member as well. Both of his parents were successful in that they had relocated to the North from the South and, as every American desires, fared better than their parents.

Jimmy was well brought up to have strong morals and values. We both were. And we attempted to instill those same values in our children. My family had admiration for Jimmy. He had a lot of personality and he hit it off with my sisters. Even my brothers— who were naturally protective of me and felt no man was good enough for me—became fond of Jimmy.

One of my brothers even pulled me aside and said, "I think that Jimmy is all right!" That was a real compliment coming from my most protective brother.

Jimmy respected my parents and never did anything to upset them when we were dating. He would always see that I was home by the designated hour. Sometimes that meant taking me home and continuing on with his evening/night out. I remember, on his prom night he made sure that I got home in time for my curfew and then went back out with his friends. And that was fine because I trusted Jimmy.

About a year into our marriage, I noticed another side of Jimmy. At times we would enjoy spooning, which is natural for most couples. But every now and then, he would put a pillow or the covers between us so that our bodies wouldn't touch. That hurt but I never said anything. Perhaps that was Mr. Proper, James.

The next night, he would be romantic and loving and I would forget about the pillow or the covers that he put between us the night before. Jimmy always had that way about him. Just when I would feel like I had had it and couldn't take it anymore, he would do something and somehow everything would seem okay.

He would be nice for a minute and then he would put a grip on me and turn back to his old ways, like Dr. Jekyll and Mr. Hyde. Perhaps the split personality came from his struggle with his bisexuality. Perhaps in his mind, Jimmy was the family man, the loving father and husband. And this "J" person was the wild, swinging homosexual.

When we first got married, Jimmy and I used to

stay up some nights after making love and talk into the wee hours of the morning. We shared our deepest thoughts (or so I thought). He once told me that he had a fantasy world that he enjoyed. In this world he is single, drives a sports car, and is a jet-setter, traveling all over the world. I was hurt by his fantasy because the children and I weren't in it.

I knew he loved to travel and be free. That's why he joined the military. And while I was hurt, I didn't think. I figured that his family was normal. We had normal dreams. We wanted a nice home—which we had. He wanted a nice car, which we planned on getting. We wanted to be able to put our children in the finest of schools and pay for college. I also knew that Jimmy wanted a wife who represented him, who was attentive to him. I felt like he really wanted me to be there for his every whim and be behind him. And I fulfilled that. I did everything he asked—even dressed the way he wanted.

But it wasn't enough. He wanted more. Perhaps he needed more. And that desire made him seethe inside. It turned him into a different person.

After I discovered he was living a double life and ended our marriage, he did some very nasty and vindictive things to get back at me. In his mind he had convinced himself and even some of our friends that I had done him wrong. He did a complete one-eighty.

People do crazy things when they want to be vindictive. He thought I should stay. He felt like I was his possession, that I was *his* wife. I guess he felt I should have reacted the way I normally reacted when he did something that displeased me—just let it roll off my back. Anything he did or said was okay with me. But this time, I asserted myself. I took action and he didn't know how to handle it.

At first he tried to win me back, but when that didn't work, he turned mean.

One day I came home and all four tires on my car were flat—the air had been let out—and I discovered that the cable wire had been cut. Jimmy never admitted to doing these things; it was just strange. And he was acting very strange during this time.

When he came back to get the rest of his things, he took a lot of souvenirs that I had collected from overseas. These were items that had sentimental value to me and he knew this. These were things that I liked. He didn't care about the trinkets; he just wanted to hurt me. I would see these things in his mother's house collecting dirt when I would go there on Sundays to pick up the kids. But I let it go.

As soon as I was one hundred percent sure I was making the right decision in divorcing him, Jimmy would turn around and do something so nice or behave in such a sweet way that I would have second thoughts.

The first time we had a civil conversation after the divorce was almost two years after the night I threw him out. He was living in an apartment in Columbus,

Ohio, and the kids spent the weekend with him. I drove there to pick up the kids and he invited me out to dinner with them. We went to Flaky Jake's—a local chain restaurant that the kids loved. It was like old times. He was overly nice and sweet. And for a moment, I forgot about our problems, about the deception. It just felt nice to be a family again.

"Maybe this can work," crept into my mind. "Maybe he *can* change."

I was very lonely. Jimmy was the first and only man I had ever been with, and it was hard for me even to think about being with anyone else, let alone trust another man again. At the same time, sitting at dinner with the kids and Jimmy brought back old memories and made me yearn for those days when we were the perfect family.

Sitting at the table looking at us as a family, I thought about it. It was up to me. He wanted me back. At least it seemed that way. It was a nice day. I thought I could rekindle that old flame—for the kids and for me. I liked being married. I like the comforts of a relationship, a home, a two-parent home. I didn't want to be a single mother, a divorcée. I liked being a wife. That's what I grew up knowing and that's what I felt my children deserved.

After dinner, we went back to Jimmy's apartment. While the kids were getting their things together, Jimmy and I sat in the living room. We got real cozy. He made a move to kiss me. I wanted him to kiss me and I allowed him to kiss me. After the kiss, I guess I remembered the lies, the other men, and I snapped back to reality. I realized then that there was nothing to rekindle. There was no spark left. It was empty.

I pulled away and the kids came out and we left. During the hour drive back to Springfield, I truly came to grips with being alone. I started entertaining my life without him. That Jimmy was gone forever.

Chapter 7

"YES, HE'S GAY!"

Throughout my life, I have grappled with my own identity, who I am. As a young child, I often felt ambivalent about myself, in fact, confused.

By virtue of my traditions, and my community, I worked hard to ensure that I was accepted as part of the traditional family of America . . .

Yet, from my early days in school, until the present day, I acknowledged some feelings, a certain sense that separated me from others. But because of my resolve, and also thinking that I was doing the right thing, I forced what I thought was an acceptable reality onto myself, a reality which is layered and layered with all the, quote, good things, and all the, quote, right things of typical adolescent and adult behavior.

Yet, at my most reflective, maybe even spiritual level, there were points in my life when I began to question what an acceptable reality really meant for me. Were there realities from which I was running?

Which master was I trying to serve?

I do not believe that God tortures any person simply for its own sake. I believe that God enables all things to work for the greater good. And this, the 47th year of my life, is arguably too late to have this discussion. But it is here, and it is now.

At a point in every person's life, one has to look deeply into the mirror of one's soul and decide one's unique truth in the world, not as we may want to see it or hope to see it, but as it is.

And so my truth is that I am a gay American . . .

CNN.com Aug. 13, 2004

These words were delivered by Jim McGreevy, the governor of New Jersey, on August 12, 2004. He was announcing his resignation from office. These words must have liberated thousands of homosexuals throughout the country. It was a watershed moment, giving men and women across the country license to follow his lead, license to be true to themselves.

For me, the moment was bittersweet. I had for so

long lived with someone who was obviously struggling with the same demons, obviously battling the same fears, who could not and would not ever admit it.

Jim McGreevy's words—"And so my truth is that I am a gay American"—would have provided so much relief to me if uttered by my then husband, Jimmy (known now as J.L.) King. That's all I wanted to hear. It would have cleared up so many years of doubt and despair, so much confusion, and so many questions. Those words would have validated what I had suspected as true.

But I never heard those words. And I am resigned that I never will.

I doubt we will ever see a prominent, powerful, or even popular black man stand up and say the things Jim McGreevy said. And I know for a fact that there are many men living a double life, living a lie. There will not be a press conference or a confession made, because even in this day and age, to be gay in the black community—especially for a leader in the community—is a fate worse than death.

Jim McGreevy, former governor of New Jersey, is a white man. While he was raised a Catholic, in politics, and leading a life where an announcement like the one he made would seemingly mean the end, for him, it may be the beginning. Jim McGreevy lives in a world of *Will & Grace,* of *Six Feet Under,* of *Queer Eye for the Straight Guy.* In Jim McGreevy's world, being gay is not the end of the world. It is more accepted now in communities throughout the country than it has ever been.

Even though there is still widespread hatred of gays within the Christian right, the white world provides a haven and support groups for homosexuals. There is a place for people like Jim McGreevy. There are no places for people like Jimmy or J.L. King or for so many other brothers on the "down low."

I don't believe there is such a thing as being "down low." To men, the so-called down low brothers are homosexual men who are afraid to admit that they love and prefer sex with men. They don't want to be considered "gay." They fool themselves by saying, "I'm not really a homosexual, I just happen to have sex with a man—it's what I do, it's not who I am."

No, if you have sex with a man, you are gay—you are a homosexual. I understand the need not to be identified with that lifestyle. But there is a greater need, I believe, for men to be truthful and honest— with their loved ones and especially with themselves. And that truth will set them free.

Only then—only after admitting the truth—can true healing begin. I believe we have so many problems in the black community, so many cases of HIV and AIDS, so many other diseases and heartaches, because people are not honest about who they are. And this problem transcends sex. But when it comes to sex, the lies can grow deadly.

The years following my discovery that my husband

was living a double life and having sex with men while in our marriage were some of the scariest years I have spent. I constantly worried about whether I had contracted the HIV virus, although I was also too afraid to actually find out. I was afraid to get involved with another man because I wondered, "Is he gay, too?" and "How can I really tell?"

I understand why DL men need to have a cover girl, to have a "wife" or a "woman" on their arm to mask their true desires. I understand. But these men must consider the harm they are doing, not only to these women but to themselves.

For Jim McGreevy, it cost him his career. A man was able to blackmail him because he knew that McGreevy would never want his "secret" to become public. But McGreevy took back his power by making the announcement, "I am a gay American!" You can't blackmail someone with something he is willing to make public himself.

And while I do not condone the lifestyle and I do believe that homosexuality is a sin, I do not judge. I would rather men and women who have these proclivities to just be up front about them. Imagine if a prominent black politician, sports figure, national leader, or businessman stepped forward and admitted he was gay. And if he was joined by a few more, would there not be a level of acceptance? Would there not be some comfort with being honest?

I believe there would be.

Jimmy and I grew up in the same community with the same homophobia. There was always some comment about a "punk" or someone who was "funny" in our community. And while we all knew someone in our church, in our school, or even in our family who might have been gay, no one ever talked about it publicly. And it was never, ever accepted as okay. And if you grew up in a community where you would be held to ridicule, reduced to nothing, ignored, or shunned, you would lie and run and hide, too.

It takes a lot of courage to come out of the closet. It takes a big man to admit something like that. I wish there were more big men out there. It would spare a lot of lives.

I'm not saying that it's okay to sin. I am saying that we cannot shun someone for being a homosexual any more than we shun someone for being a drug addict. We try to help a drug addict; we try to help someone who is struggling with a problem; we don't ostracize them because then they will simply run and not ever get help.

Society—particularly the black community—has spent so much time making people feel uncomfortable or like lepers for being what they feel is the way they were created that we have driven people so far into the closet that they have made up a whole new identity—the DL. What people on the down low say is, "I'm not gay!" They say that having sex with people of the same sex is simply something they do, but it doesn't define who they are. They are not gay because they say so. But that's not true. And not only are they lying to people around them, they are lying to themselves.

The lying would be fine if they weren't taking lives with those lies. By not owning up to being gay, they completely ignore the reports that come out about homosexuals and the risks of homosexual behavior because they believe those warnings don't apply to them. They're not gay. Even if a man truly wants to overcome his problem, he will never be able to if he does not first admit to being a homosexual.

The first step in all twelve-step programs for people battling addictions is to first admit you have a problem. Men (and women) living on the DL won't admit it. Jimmy denied to me that he was having sex with men and still hasn't admitted it to me face-to-face. If he hadn't written it in his book, I think he still would be trying to deny it to me. And as long as they are lying and hiding, they won't get any help.

On the other hand, there are men and women who are happy being homosexual and very proud of it. That's who they are. It is insulting for someone who is living in their world to lie about it. A lot of homosexuals are angry with Jimmy because they feel that he is casting a negative light on them. They feel that women will blame them for the things people living on the DL are doing. And I understand the anger. They are taking the risks and living their lives in an up-front manner and here come these DL men, perpetrating and leaving the homosexual men holding the bag on the AIDS epidemic—when, in fact, the DL men are responsible for spreading the virus among women.

From my spiritual perspective, I believe that homosexuality is a sin. And I believe that if people are willing, they can be delivered from it.

In the summer of 2004, Donnie McClurkin, Grammy award-winning gospel singer and a pastor from New York, admitted that he is a "reformed bisexual."

"I was involved one time in bisexuality, but it was God that delivered me from that," McClurkin told *New York Daily News* "Lowdown" columnist Lloyd Grove on August 29, 2004. "There is a way out, there is change, there is another way."

For McClurkin, being a homosexual or a bisexual is a choice. If someone is a kleptomaniac and feels compelled to steal, he or she has to control those urges because it is illegal and a thief can go to jail. I believe that people have urges but that a mature person and especially someone who follows the ways of God can control, suppress, and even change those urges.

There are people who battle with eating disorders. But there is counseling for them, and that's acceptable. There are people who battle with drug addiction, and there are programs and counseling for them, and that's acceptable and even encouraged. But when a man talks about battling his homosexual urges, people roll their eyes. If you go online, there are many blogs and commentary on Donnie McClurkin's admission of his past and his move to do something about it. Many people ridicule him; some even vilify him for saying he has overcome it, as if to say that's not possible.

But I applaud Donnie McClurkin. And I say he gives hope to thousands of people who are struggling. And unlike too many preachers and pastors and ministers and priests and rabbis, McClurkin is putting the issue on Front Street and forcing people, including his congregation, to deal with it.

"There is a way out, there is change, there is another way," said McClurkin, who is a father of a young son and is a pastor of the Perfecting Faith nondenominational church in Freeport, Long Island. "Those that want help, I am here to help."

Those who want help have to first admit that they need help. For some, homosexuality is not something they want to be delivered from and that's their prerogative. But those people owe it to their loved ones to be completely honest about their sexual habits and to be honest with themselves. Those who have sex with the same sex must look in the mirror and say, "I am gay! I am a homosexual."

And those who are embarrassed and hate the things they do and who want to be delivered from homosexuality must also be honest and look in the mirror and tell themselves, "I am gay! I am a homosexual."

And then they need to go to a church or a pastor who understands and get help. The pastor of the church I was attending when I was married to Jimmy did not understand. But there are many wonderful churches and pastors that help people make a transition from a life of sin to one of light and salvation.

Now that I have found such a church and am myself in the ministry, I understand that the pastor who told me to go back to Jimmy and "be a better wife" to him wasn't trying to hurt me. He gave me that advice because he didn't want to instruct me to leave my husband. He didn't want to be culpable for our divorce. It was easier for him to tell me to stay than to have to really counsel me—and Jimmy—and deal with the truth.

Ministers have to understand that real leadership means saying the tough things to people and telling the truth—even if it hurts. When a woman talks to me about her marriage and her husband who is doing wrong, I instruct her to go to a professional who has no ties to her, her marriage, or her husband. I tell her to seek clergy who are well informed and trained in her area of need. Sometimes it means doing a little research, asking around for people who have gotten good results. But you can't always do it on your own. Having someone there for you to see you through it— especially someone who has solid spiritual grounding—will make the road a lot easier to travel.

And for the men who are lying to their wives or

girlfriends and who are leading secret lives and feel that they cannot stop, I know that they can. If they truly want to stop, there is help for them, too. It makes no sense to destroy the lives of so many so-called love ones—the wife, the kids, the parents. It makes no sense to run and hide and lie. Get help.

Chapter 8

OH GOD!

The bombshell dropped by Pastor Donnie Mc-Clurkin in 2004 was just the opening the black church needed to put the issue of homosexuality, bisexuality, and AIDS on the forefront of its agenda.

During the Civil Rights Movement, the black church was instrumental in leading boycotts and motivating its members to march and protest on behalf of voting rights and equal treatment. It was the efforts of pastors and preachers throughout the South that applied the pressure for change. It was their sacrifice and their vision that forced this nation to take stock of where it was and then change the direction in which they were going.

Dr. Martin Luther King Jr. delivered his most compelling speeches from the pulpits of churches throughout this country. He was a minister, a pastor with the courage to take on the system even at his own peril. He helped bring his people out of the darkness and into a new existence. Dr. King was a revolutionary. He was a pioneer.

There is a need for another type of pioneer in the church today. Donnie McClurkin opened the door in 2004 by admitting his own struggles with "bisexuality" and by talking about overcoming it. It's time for other ministers to step up.

It makes no sense that so many preachers stand in the pulpit on Sunday morning preaching from the Book of Romans and talking about what an abomination homosexuality is and never address what is going on within the walls of that church. It makes no sense for the sermons of fire and brimstone, hell and damnation, to be delivered when right there next to the pulpit, sitting in front of the church, is the choir director who is as gay as the day is long. But no one says anything. Or the pastor himself is a homosexual who hypocritically preaches against homosexuals in the day yet dabbles in it himself at night.

We have to see where that kind of hypocrisy ends. In the Catholic Church several priests have come under fire and prosecution for molesting altar boys and others who come to them for counseling. Priests take an oath of celibacy. They are not supposed to have sex of any kind. But when you run and hide and lie about who you really are, eventually it will all come out. In the Catholic Church it came out in the sexual abuse.

In the black community the dirty little secret is

even deadlier. Black women are the largest-growing risk group for HIV and AIDS because of the DL phenomenon. And the black church should take a leading role in stopping this trend. In his book, Jimmy writes about some gospel conventions, which are basically meeting places and feeding grounds for homosexual activity. The pastors don't know? The congregation doesn't know? Of course, everyone knows, but they just turn a blind eye—the way the Catholic Church ignored what so many priests were doing for so many years. It cannot go on.

I applaud Donnie McClurkin for not only admitting the truth but putting it in its proper perspective. He was quoted on the Christian Broadcasting Network's website as saying about homosexuals: "I'm not in the mood to play with those who are trying to kill our children." He should add those who are killing our women, too.

While I don't believe McClurkin is vilifying homosexuals, he is talking from his heart about what he knows is the truth. You can't play with fire and not get burned. This is not a subject you can preach about and not deal with the day-to-day realities. And what better person to speak on it than someone who was once in that life? Who better to understand?

When I was struggling with my discovery that my husband was sleeping with a man and I went to my pastor, I wasn't met with understanding. My pastor wasn't trying to hear what I was saying or where I was coming from. He gave me a "solution" that might have killed me. He told me to go back home and be a better wife to my husband.

He told me that I would burn in hell for wrongly accusing my husband. He told me to go home and pray. And I did. I prayed. I prayed that God would show me the truth—that He would confirm for me what I knew in my spirit already—that Jimmy was having an affair with a man. And God did reveal that truth.

We are taught that the truth will set us free, but many of us never want to face the truth. It's too painful. The truth is that God's word is clear about how He feels about sin. And homosexuality is a sin. You cannot be a pulpit minister and be a practicing homosexual. That is completely against the Word.

In August 2003, the House of Bishops voted to make Gene Robinson a bishop in the Episcopal Church. He became the first openly gay bishop in the church's history. He and his partner (lover) stood at the ceremony beaming. And I thought, "How can this be? What God do they serve? And what bible do they read?"

I will not judge or speak out against anyone who is gay. But I draw the line at the pulpit. I believe people of the cloth should be held to a higher standard. I cannot believe that a homosexual is called to preach.

But once again, in the interest of being politically correct, they allow it because they don't want to be judgmental. But what does the Bible say? What does God say? And how can you lead and teach and promote the word of God when you openly live counter to that word?

In 2004 the issue of gay marriage made its way to the forefront. Again, if people want to get married, that's fine. But the church is not the place for that. Churches and church leaders should not be opening their doors to perform these weddings. You don't have to speak out against it as a minister, but you shouldn't be condoning it.

Former Democratic presidential nominee John Kerry held a rally at the Greater Grace Temple in Springfield, Ohio, in July 2004. Actually, Kerry said he was simply attending service there but it turned into a rally. I attended the service, too. And outside the church was a man passing out literature. The title of one of his handouts was "God's Opinion on Homosexuality and Gay Marriage." In it, there was a breakdown on God's views of homosexuality as they are laid out in the bible.

There were a lot of harsh scriptures referenced about how God views homosexuality as an abomination, and I am certain for those who are struggling with homosexuality, that's the last thing you want to hear. And I understand. But you cannot serve two masters. You cannot sit in church every Sunday or preach from the pulpit every Sunday or direct the choir every Sunday and claim to be a follower of God and go home and practice homosexuality. There is a conflict there. And ignoring that conflict won't resolve it.

At the same time, those who are not homosexual but who see it in the church can't ignore it either. Nor can they point fingers and condemn people—that's not their role. We must treat sinners the way Jesus treated the woman who was going to be stoned for committing adultery. We must deal with everyone with love and understanding, yet at the same time hold them accountable to the Word.

I don't agree with gay marriage. And as far as homosexuality, I know it is a fact of life but I believe that a person can be delivered from it just like from any other sin. I also believe that no sin is greater than any other sin. Bearing false witness, murder, and lust are all equal in the eyes of God. Sin is sin.

I recently met a man at a function in Springfield, where I gave a speech. He approached me after hearing my story and finding out that my ex-husband wrote the *Down Low* book. He said he felt uneasy and unsure of himself for years, but after reading *On the Down Low,* he felt released and free to talk about being molested as a child. He said he was gay. He had never talked about this before with anyone. I asked him if he had not been molested, would he have chosen this lifestyle. After some thought, he said, "No."

I felt sad for him. My heart went out for him and all of the people who have had horrible things happen to them as a child. Children imitate what they see and experience. I believe he was impressionable as a child and thought this was the way to live. People who are abusive, research has found, generally grew up in abusive homes. You would think, after experiencing it growing up, that abuse would be the last thing someone would want to repeat, but that's exactly what happens. And children who are sexually abused, oftentimes grow up to be abusers. And little boys who are abused by men tend to emulate the behavior, and some grow up to be gay. I cannot explain why people imitate things so hateful and hurtful; I just know that they do.

There are too many adults in our society who prey on children and take their innocence. This young man started to cry and get emotional as he shared his story with me. We cried together. He asked me for a hug, and I gave him the biggest hug I could muster. He said that being molested kept him from intimacy; it kept him from having a normal relationship.

I know this young man is not alone. I also know that God can deliver him.

I hear those who say, "I was born this way." And "God doesn't make mistakes." God doesn't make mistakes. But God gave us all free will. He gave us all challenges in our lives to overcome. He put things in our path that, while we didn't ask for them, we are expected to handle according to his Word. Some people are born missing an arm or a leg or are born blind, yet they have to live their lives and overcome. So if you believe you were born gay, yet the Bible says that it is a sin, you must fight your nature and not sin. You have to overcome it and you can. Ask Donnie McClurkin.

Chapter 9

HE DOESN'T GIVE YOU
MORE . . .

In the winter of 1989 we had an ice storm. The streets and sidewalks of Springfield were filled with ice and snow. I needed to go to the grocery for a few items to prepare my family's dinner. Against my husband Loren's wishes, I bundled up to go out to start the car. Ice was on the patio leading to the driveway where the car was parked. It was not parked in the garage that evening.

Right before I got to the car, my foot slipped on the hidden ice and I fell. My husband and children ran out to the car after they heard me scream. My husband checked to see if I was okay and picked me up off the ground, reminding me that he'd told me it was too icy to leave the house.

After the fall I noticed that my balance was not quite right. At times I felt like I was slowly spinning. I also had a numbness running through my hands and feet. I tried to ignore whatever was going on in my body, figuring it would be all right. But it got worse. Slowly I began to lose the use of my arms and hands. Small tasks like cooking, washing dishes, and other household chores became difficult.

I began to notice that I couldn't write or use a keyboard without it being a big effort. I was promoted to an administrative position within the welfare department at this point and was doing a lot of paperwork. Holding a pen was even difficult.

I would drop things in the kitchen and couldn't write my reports at work. Something was wrong. But I tried to mask it so that my family wouldn't worry.

I made an appointment with the doctor after my sister-in-law suggested that my symptoms resembled those of an older sister of mine who had multiple sclerosis. She later died of breast cancer. I was reluctant to have the test done because I didn't want to know if something was really wrong. But I had to find out for my family's sake.

It was confirmed that I had MS. I was admitted into the hospital to endure a series of tests that ranged from magnetic resonance imaging (MRI) to a spinal tap—which was extremely painful. The neurologist who took the spinal tap had to try two times on two different days to get it right, to find the right spot for the spinal fluid. I had to hold perfectly still and lie in a fetal position while he inserted a very long needle into my spine.

For me that was worse than childbirth. I gave birth

to all of my children naturally, no drugs. I was very fortunate because I was never in labor longer than three hours. Ebony was born an hour after my labor began. So the spinal tap was a new level of pain.

The MRI was scary, too. The lab that I went to didn't have open MRI so I had to be led through this dark, tight tube and was told to remain still or else the test would not come out accurately. I felt like I would suffocate. I discovered that day that I am claustrophobic. The test, which lasts for only an hour, seemed like it took half a day.

I was not as anxious waiting for the results of my test as my family was. I knew that the results would be positive, that I would be found to have MS. I have always been pretty in tune with my body and read up on the disease. There was no other explanation for the symptoms I was experiencing.

My stay in the hospital lasted about a week. My husband stepped in to take care of the kids while I was in the hospital. He did all of the housework, the cooking and cleaning, even after I came home. I couldn't use my hands. Writing out a check became impossible for me. Loren had to go to the grocery store and pay the bills, which had been my job. He said that the best part of this stage of my illness and my inability to use my hands was that he got to bathe me. He seemed to get a kick out of that. Bless his heart!

But I was frustrated. I had become pretty independent, and I hated people doing things for me. And I definitely didn't want to be a burden to anyone. But sometimes in life you have to just let go. I didn't have a choice.

After finding out that I had MS, my greatest fear was not being active with my children. I tried to explain my illness to the children as best I could with the little knowledge I had so that they could understand it. The problem was that even the medical professionals did not fully understand MS.

There are so many different stages of the disease and it affects everyone differently. Multiple sclerosis is an unpredictable disease of the central nervous system (brain and spinal cord) in which the insulating, protective covering (myelin sheath) surrounding the nerves is destroyed. This destruction results in an interference with the ways the brain signals various parts of the body. Hard or firm scar tissue replaces the areas where the myelin is lost, hence the name *multiple sclerosis* (multiple scars). MS can range from relatively benign, to somewhat disabling, to devastating, as communication between the brain and other parts of the body is disrupted.

For talk show host and motivational speaker Montel Williams, MS doesn't appear to be devastating. He was diagnosed in 1999 and has been a very vocal and visible poster person for the disease. He works out every day and has changed his diet. And while he has his bad days, Montel Williams is definitely living with MS. It has not hampered his career.

For Lola Falana, who was one of the hottest acts of

the 1970s and 1980s, MS ended her career when she was stricken with it in 1987. She could no longer do her show-stopping, high-energy Las Vegas performances. She couldn't sing or dance. The doctors said there was nothing they could do for her so she did what people should always do—turn to God.

"God was trying to get my attention but I wasn't listening," Lola Falana said in an interview. "It took Him allowing me to have MS to get my attention."

The disease crippled her. She was bound to a wheelchair and blind. But through prayer and faith she was healed. In 1990 she made her way back to the Las Vegas stage.

"I wanted to say farewell," she said. "I wanted to show the world that God had healed me, and that if I chose to continue performing, that I could continue. However, I chose to go from a star to a servant of Jesus Christ."

I also believe that God was trying to get my attention. I had spent so much of my life serving others and doing for others that for the first time, I was forced to let people do for me. It was tough. I was saddest about giving up my active life. Loren and I were very active with the kids. Our favorite activity was cycling with them. But I had no balance to walk, let alone navigate on a bicycle.

After a couple of weeks, I was determined to resume my work. I didn't allow MS to be an excuse for me. I continued to cook, clean, and eventually went back to work. Simple tasks took more effort, took longer, and made me tire sooner, but I pushed through.

I was put on drugs, steroids that gave me strength, but I began to put on a great deal of weight and it gave me a moon face. I hated the medicine. Again, I didn't take drugs even to give birth. I was determined to stop taking the drugs and not to be defeated.

I remember sitting on the side of the bed with my husband after coming home from the hospital and just crying in his arms that I wanted to see my children grown. My husband was very supportive and comforting, but I could see the fear in his eyes. I was afraid of what might happen. I didn't know if MS was chronic or even fatal. All I could do was put it in God's hands. I prayed that God would restore my strength and let me continue to enjoy my family, both immediate and extended.

I would not allow people to feel sorry for me. And I refused to feel sorry for myself. I had faith that God would see me through.

When I told my mother of my diagnosis, she said, "I wonder what I did?" She thought that, after having two daughters who were diagnosed with MS, she had perhaps done something while she was pregnant with us. Or perhaps she felt that she hadn't done something necessary for our health while we were growing up. She was another woman taking the blame, feeling responsible.

My father, who was alive at the time, also set me back a bit. He told me that I could use a wheelchair that he had in the garage if I needed it. I was very offended. How dare he think I would ever need a wheelchair! I knew he meant well and was only trying to be helpful, but I wasn't even considering a wheelchair and I didn't want anyone around me considering it either.

I was going to keep walking. I didn't care how slow I had to take it at first. Sometimes the people who love you the most can deliver the harshest blow when you are attempting to overcome something in your life.

I was eventually weaned off the medicine and became stronger on my own, praise God! I haven't been on any medicine since. And after about a year, if I didn't tell you I had MS, you would not have known that anything was wrong with me. I started riding my bike again with my children. I started hiking again with my husband. And I continued to do everything that I enjoyed doing.

In August 2004, a month before my birthday, I had a series of tests, including another MRI. When the doctor came in to give me the results, he asked me, "Did I tell you that you had multiple sclerosis?" I said yes. "Well, there is not a single trace of the disease in your system!"

I was healed.

Before getting the clean bill of health, I had taken measures to improve my health. I bought *The Multiple Sclerosis Diet Book,* by Roy Laver Swank, M.D., Ph.D., and Barbara Brewer Dugan. After reading the book, I decided the best thing for me to do was eliminate most meats. I was not a big meat eater anyway, so I stopped eating red meat and pork. I also cut down on my fat intake. I started walking more for exercise. And to strengthen my hands I began crocheting and doing needlepoint. These two crafts were great for my hands. I adapted even though my hands were numb, which came in handy because I stuck myself several times with the needlepoint needle and didn't feel it.

One of my favorite pastimes before the illness was baking. I had to stop in the beginning because it required so much hand power. But I began baking again. It was difficult for me to roll out dough for my pie crust. I have a home bakery and make pies and cobblers. At the time that I had been diagnosed with MS, my pies were a second job for me. At holiday time, especially Thanksgiving and Christmas, many people would request my pies and cobblers for their family gatherings. I was happy to oblige and this also paid for my family's holidays.

The first time I tried to bake a pie again, I couldn't hold the rolling pin. But again I was determined. I ended up positioning the rolling pin on my wrists and rolled the dough. The pie turned out excellent.

To strengthen my legs I would take walks at the lake on a walking trail. My left leg would tire easily and start to drag, but I kept on walking. All of this self-determination and faith that God would restore my strength is what led to my healing. I believed in healing. I believed that God gives us wisdom not to pollute and blatantly defile our temple. There is enough in the world that can happen to our bodies when we are taking care of them so why add to the destruction by blatantly abusing our bodies with drugs, alcohol, unprotected sex, and overeating.

This process of battling MS and becoming healthy was the second time that I took matters into my hands and allowed God to work for me. The first time was leaving Jimmy. God empowers you when you make moves to empower yourself.

I also learned that God tests you and sometimes obstacles are thrown in your path to see how you will handle them. Will you curl up and do nothing, or will you roll up your sleeves and overcome?

I had to endure the loss of my twins, which was one of the most devastating things to happen to me. I dealt with my husband's betrayal and I overcame. Before battling MS, my best friend Roxanne died suddenly of an enlarged heart. She was thirty-five years old.

After that, I realized how short life really is and how much we owe it to ourselves and to God to do with our lives as much as we possibly can. I knew I couldn't waste my time living for someone else—be it my parents or my husband or even my children. I made a conscious decision to live for Brenda.

The first thing I did was quit my job. I had worked

for Human Services in Springfield for twelve years. I had been skipped over for promotions for years. The last straw was when I was skipped over for a woman whom I had trained in the new program for Family and Children's Services Information System (FACSIS). I understood the system that I worked for. But I also realized that there was no place for me to go there. So instead of being frustrated and hurt, I moved on.

I had quit college when Jimmy and I had gotten married in order to travel with him while he was in the service. I had recently remarried and now realized that it was time to live for Brenda and live out those goals and dreams. I reenrolled at Central State University in Wilberforce, Ohio, and began studies in journalism/communications. I had a wonderful professor, Dr. Emil Dansker, who called the nontraditional older students "Retreads." Omarosa from *The Apprentice* was in my class with Dr. Dansker. He was instrumental in both of our careers.

Had it not been for the many life-changing moments from the death of my friend to the MS diagnosis, I doubt if I would have had the "throw caution to the wind" mentality to finish my college degree. It had been a lifelong goal. I was the last of eight children, six living, to get my degree. My only regret is that my parents were not able to see me receive my diploma, since graduation from college had been their goal for all their children. My mother, who was suffering from Parkinson's disease, was an invalid, and my father, her caretaker, was battling the early stages of lung cancer and did not feel well enough to attend my graduation ceremony. My mother had not attended my high school graduation either, because of illness.

After graduation I decided to start a new career. I worked for a newspaper and for the city school system as a substitute teacher, which was very fulfilling, more so than the newspaper reporting. I felt like I was making a difference in the lives of children. I did both for a while and also continued my education at Urbana University in Urbana, Ohio, to work toward a degree in education. My thirst for knowledge didn't stop there. I think that is the nature of a journalist; we are interested in everything. That thirst is always there. And once you are faced with a life-changing illness, you begin to embrace life with a new zeal.

There was something stirring in me. I took time to reflect on my life and I realized there was a greater purpose for me than being a journalist or even teaching. I had a calling.

When my father was dying of lung cancer, he was lying in bed barely able to talk and seeming restless. I didn't know what to do or to say. I read him the Twenty-Third Psalm, and it seemed to bring him peace. To this day I live my life by the Twenty-Third Psalm.

God is my refuge. I put my trust, my life, in God's

hands. God has led me in directions that I could not fathom. I continue to let God lead my life. He led me into my ministry, which is geared to help and guide women who have experienced similar situations as I have in their lives.

Chapter 10

THE GUIDE

First, I need to clarify that the term *down low* can refer to any lying, cheating man—not just a man who is sleeping with other men. Any man who is lying to you can put your life in jeopardy.

Before you start dealing with that, however, you need to make sure your man is on the down low. My pastor was right about one thing—falsely accusing someone is one of the worst things you can do.

Often when there are problems in a relationship, people want to point fingers. Before investigating your man, you need to check yourself. Take a good look in the mirror and make sure that *you* are not the problem. Make sure that you are living up to your end of the relationship.

Before I faced off with Jimmy, I had concrete evidence. That is the only thing that kept me strong through his denials and lies—I knew for sure that he was cheating on me. I knew he was sleeping with a man.

Once you have checked yourself and the problem isn't you and you discover that you are indeed dealing with a down low man, there are a few things you can do to protect yourself and keep yourself sane.

1. Love and respect yourself.

This is almost kryptonite for a man living on the down low. Men who have something to hide tend to run far away from women who are self-confident and who love themselves. Men on the DL are looking for a woman who will allow them to get away with their secret lives.

If a woman loves herself and knows who she is, this will make it more difficult getting connected with a man who is a liar. And if you do find yourself involved with a man on the down low, a strong sense of self and self-confidence will give you the strength to make the tough choices. If you love yourself, you will be less likely to allow someone to continue to lie to you, to cheat on you, to abuse you.

Getting respect begins with respecting yourself. If you honor yourself, others will honor you.

2. Follow your instincts.

Mother Nature gave every woman a sixth sense. My mother called it "mother wit." Others call it intuition. If you are in tune with yourself, your intuition will rarely fail you.

I knew something was wrong with my relationship with Jimmy. I was unwilling to listen to that internal voice. I was afraid of what she was telling me to do because at the time I wasn't willing to do it. I chose to ignore that little voice, ignore my intuition, and follow my heart, which was telling me that the man I loved would never do anything to hurt me. I loved him and he loved me.

But my inner voice was telling me something different. It wasn't until I was forced to come face-to-face with the truth that I responded. But the signs were there all along. The same signs that I ignored back then look so obvious to me today.

3. Don't wallow in self-pity; do something!

Even the strongest, securest woman can get caught out there with a man on the down low. But it's what that woman does next that defines her.

Some will argue that it takes a lot of strength to stay with a man who has done you wrong. I disagree. I think it takes strength to leave. It takes strength to say, "No more!" It takes strength to say, "Get out!" and mean it—not letting him ever back in. That's the hard part for many women. It was hard for me.

But I knew if I was going to respect myself, he had to go. Somewhere inside I knew, despite his claims, that everything was fine and that we could be happy again. Jimmy was not going to change. I'm not saying that a person cannot change. But they need to do their changing apart from you and prove it.

For me, staying with Jimmy would not only kill my self-esteem, but would be sending the wrong message to my kids. Despite what many parents think, kids know more than they let on. They see and hear things we don't think they see and hear. And they definitely understand more than we give them credit for. I didn't want my daughter ever to make the same mistakes that I made. And I didn't want her to see her mother stay in a situation that wasn't good for her. That wasn't the example that I wanted to set for my daughter.

For my son, I wanted to make sure that he knew how to treat a woman well. I didn't want him to think it was okay for a man to mistreat a woman. Staying would have sent him that message.

Before entering into a relationship, you must be a whole person. You must know that you are a complete person by yourself, that a man will not complete you. He will not make you a woman; you must come to him as a woman, and he must come to you as a man. Having a man in your life adds to your life; it does not make you less of a woman not to have a man. God made you fearfully and wonderfully and on purpose, an individual.

4. Seek counsel.

I don't mean an attorney, although one may be necessary in the end. I mean find someone to confide in. Don't do like many women do—run out and tell everyone who will listen to your problems. This, I believe, creates more problems, and it rarely helps you get through what you're going through.

But you must find someone you can trust—a professional counselor, a compassionate and loving pastor, or a very, very close friend—whom you can sound off and vent to.

Silence can be deadly. Your silence can kill not only your spirit but the spirit of those around you. I have met so many women who come up to me and say, "I thought I was all alone. I didn't think anyone else was going through what I was going through." They have spent so many years holding back the pain and keeping it inside that they are broken. And as a result, their family is broken. The woman, in many ways, is the backbone of the family. Once she breaks, the whole family can crumble.

I, too, suffered in silence, too embarrassed to tell anyone. And when I did decide to tell someone—my pastor—I was knocked for a loop. I was also embarrassed because I somehow thought it might be my fault. I didn't want to be judged as a bad wife.

But I have learned that sharing your story helps you heal. I had two close friends—one my sister-in-law—who helped me get through my bad times. They were the ones who listened to me when I needed to talk, who provided that shoulder to cry on when I needed it. They didn't judge me. Even then, I didn't share everything that I should have and it haunted me for years.

They say when you keep things, you can make yourself sick. The medical profession has attributed all kinds of ailments from ulcers to cancer to holding on to things and keeping them bottled up inside. But if it doesn't get you physically, it will definitely get you spiritually—which can be worse.

Chapter 11

SINS OF THE FATHER

One of the hardest things I had to do in dealing with the whole Jimmy ordeal was telling the children. I tried not to tell them anything as long as I could. I gave them the little "Mommy and Daddy aren't going to be living together" talk. And they accepted that.

Their lives didn't change dramatically because their routine was still the same. They still spent Sundays with Jimmy's mother, and because he lived nearby initially, they still got to see him a lot. When I married Loren, they would spend a lot of summers with Jimmy. So while we weren't together, we never stopped being their parents.

But when Ebony turned thirteen, I had to deal with "questions" about Jimmy—the dreaded questions that I never wanted to answer. I will not divulge the entirety of the conversation I had with Ebony or her reaction because that's private. But we had a tough conversation and we both came out of it okay.

One of the most important things to remember as a parent is never to break a confidence with your children. They must be able to trust you. They have to know if they tell you something that it is not going any further. Because my children trusted me, we were able to have such open and honest discussions about their father.

I know, however, that there are many mothers who are going through a relationship trial, a divorce, or a breakup where children are involved, and they are in a quandary about what to talk about. My only advice is to be honest with your children.

We do not give children enough credit. Most children know more than we could ever imagine. Ignoring the elephant in the room can lead to problems later. Just hoping they will never ask you any questions won't help your children heal. In a breakup—even the friendly ones—you aren't the only casualty. Yes, children are resilient but they gain a lot of their strength from their parents' reactions. If you are in pain, your children will certainly feel it and respond in some way—even if you don't notice it.

You children deserve some answers. But timing is everything.

Ebony was around thirteen when I noticed that she was getting interested in boys. I approached her and we had that mother-daughter talk about sex and sexual responsibility. I used the opportunity to tell her about the reason her dad and I broke up. She needed to know. I felt that she had to protect herself, and the best way to do that was through knowledge.

She listened attentively and did not seem shocked. She acted the same way that I did as a teen when my mother approached me with a book—disgusted but curious. That little talk opened the doors for Ebony to be able to talk to me about anything.

Sometimes I'm on the receiving end and I try not to act shocked. I listen and I give advice when asked for it, and I let her know that I am there for her, no matter what. I trust her and she trusts me.

We have talked more recently about men on the down low. And she knows that while there are some men out there who are lying about their sexuality, it is not the majority. Not all men are on the down low, and I tell her to use her intuition and her spirit to weed out the ones who are from those who aren't.

I am blessed because my daughter has always been very strong. She is not naive and has no problem expressing herself. And like all of my children, she believes in truth and fairness.

With Brandon, I didn't have the "perfect" opportunity to have that talk. It was stripped from me by a person who spoke before they thought. Brandon would have sleepovers with his friends and cousins throughout the year. A few summers after Jimmy and I divorced, Brandon was staying with Jimmy and wanted to have one of his friends stay over. When the little boy asked his grandmother for permission, she said, "No, Brandon's father likes men." She was close to the family and had heard the rumors and didn't want her grandson "exposed" to Jimmy. Of course, the little boy—who had stayed over with us many times—repeated it to Brandon. He was crushed.

I had to talk to him about what was said, and we talked out how he felt. Then Jimmy talked to him. He handled it all well.

When he was older, I talked with Brandon about the appropriate way to treat a woman and how he should be treated by a woman. He saw by example with me, his uncles, and my father. He has patterned himself after them, and I can say he is a good man.

For Loren, I eventually talked to him about women and the role of a man, but the talk about Jimmy didn't come until recently. It wasn't an issue that he necessarily had to deal with. Jimmy wasn't his father. I did have to say something to him before *On the Down Low* came out. I didn't want Loren finding out everything from someone else. The information didn't change how he acted around Jimmy. That was good.

Ebony, Brandon, and Loren are close and have told me that they have had some candid discussions with one another. I have always told each of them if they feel that they cannot discuss certain issues with me to please find a responsible adult who they can trust to go to for guidance. I thank God that they have each other.

I am often asked, "How do you deal with your children?" And my advice to mothers is to always tell the children, even if you have to tell them that their father is on the DL. Tell them. Explain it all and open yourself up for questions.

You would rather your child hear it from you than from someone else.

I encountered a woman whose husband was sleeping with the pastor of their church. He was the youth minister. The woman never told her children the truth about the breakup. But other family members knew the truth.

The father ended up getting killed, and the mother still hasn't told her children. I know she is afraid that someone will tell them maliciously or accidentally. But she is more afraid to tell. For all she knows, her children already know, and what must they be thinking?

Ebony asked me not to tell her brother. She said she wanted to tell him. She was protective of him. But it wasn't her place. Parents must take on the responsibility, no matter how difficult.

ON THE UP AND UP

A Survival Guide for Women Living with Men on the Down Low

by Brenda Stone Browder with Karen Hunter

ABOUT THIS GUIDE

The suggested questions are intended to enhance your group's reading of Brenda Stone Browder's book. We have also included one of Brenda's popular sermons, which we hope provides insight on Brenda's amazing journey.

Please visit Brenda's website at *www.brendabrowder.com*.

To Forgive Is Divine

I thought I had moved on. In fact, I had convinced myself that I had. I had a new life. I was even becoming more active in my church, strengthening my relationship with God. But this one Sunday revealed to me that I had some work to do. I was sitting in the pulpit with my pastor. I was the lay speaker in my church—which is the Methodist's version of a deaconess—and had read the scripture for the day. We had a visiting pastor who was preaching. His sermon was about "a defining moment." He said, "either you've been through one, you're going through one, or you're about to go through a defining moment in your life."

For some reason that sermon convicted me. And I wondered, "What defining moment am I about to go through?"

After the service was over, I was speaking to the ministers in the pulpit. Everyone was leaving the sanctuary and we were making our way down to greet the congregation. As I looked out, I locked eyes with Melvin. I had seen Melvin in church so many times since he "confessed his sins" at that altar that day. And when I did see him, I would roll my eyes, turn up my nose and go out of my way to not speak to him. If I saw him, I would walk the other way. I had so much hatred in my heart for him.

But on this day I was drawn to him. He began to approach me and I walked toward him. I had been convicted by the sermon about a defining moment and knew that I was in the midst of one. I felt a nudging from God that told me that I had to talk to this man. I had to forgive him.

When I approached him he said, "I need to ask you to forgive me." And I told him, "I need to tell you that I do forgive you." I hugged him and tears started down his face.

I felt a burden lifted from my heart. I didn't realize how much of a hypocrite I was all of those years, harboring those ill feelings and coming to church holding my head high. I had shunned this man before God. But that day I knew I had to let go of those feelings to truly move on—to truly have a new life.

I knew that I had to forgive Melvin in order to be forgiven by God. And I knew I was saved when I could look Melvin in his eyes again and see him not as a home wrecker but as a man made in the image of God.

My true healing came when I was able to face all of the hurt and anger I had bottled up over the years—

hurt and anger that I didn't even know was there—
and forgive. For many of us, that's the hardest part.
But if we are going to move on to the next place and
be truly blessed, forgiveness is a must.

I know for me, I was holding on to the past and the
old feelings like a security blanket. But like many security blankets, I had long since outgrown it—it was
worn and smelly, and it was time for it to go.

As part of my healing I stopped wallowing in my
own pit of self-pity and started thinking about others.
I got involved in things that would add to my healing
by sharing some of the things I had learned and was
learning with others.

In 2003, I unwittingly started an AIDS ministry. It
began with searching the Internet for answers, statistics, and information on AIDS. I felt the need to become educated in this subject because of what I'd
gone through. I knew that having lived with a man
who was cheating on me with men, I had been placed
at risk and I could have easily contracted the HIV
virus. There but for the grace of God go I. I felt I was
spared, delivered for a purpose, and now I was com-
missioned to do more.

While surfing the Net, I came across the "Balm in
Gilead" website. Balm in Gilead is a national organization committed to educating the public, eradicating
AIDS, and giving support to victims of this disease. It
had a plea for churches, particularly African-American
churches, to become involved in the education and
eradication of this disease.

I felt compelled to answer the call from the Balm in Gilead to make this a ministry through my church. I registered my church to become a partner. I informed my pastor that I had registered our church but at the time I had no idea where this ministry would lead. I thought, we could at least gather information through Balm in Gilead and pass it along to the congregation.

I received one phone call from a Cedarville University student looking for information on the AIDS ministry of our church. She told me that Covenant was the only church in the area registered on the Balm website. I sadly had to tell the young lady that our church was indeed a partner to the Balm, but that we did not have an active HIV/AIDS ministry.

When I mentioned HIV/AIDS to members of the church, I got an indifferent and oftentimes chilly response. Finally our pastor received a call from a member of the Delta Sigma Theta sorority, requesting that they be allowed to work with our church's HIV/AIDS ministry (which was nonexistent). They, too, had gotten the information from the Balm website that we were a partner.

The HIV/AIDS ministry began. I helped organize along with the Deltas, our church and nine churches in the city formed an interdenominational ministry for AIDS. "A Community United: Prevailing Against the Odds of AIDS" was our slogan. And it said a mouthful. Nine churches of several denominations, working together on a ministry project, was a first. It was awesome. I saw it as God's perfect design.

The Balm in Gilead national organization holds a Week of Prayer for AIDS annually and asks that all partners and churches hold programs on AIDS throughout the week. Our church partners went to work. We had no money and were concerned about where to hold the event and what to actually plan. But we came up with the money—through donations, special offerings, and even a spaghetti dinner. A Pentecostal church donated their facilities for the dinner. A Baptist church and a nondenominational church supplied liturgical/praise dancers. The nondenominational church opened their church for AIDS testing during the Week of Prayer for AIDS. Each church hosted alternating prayer and education days. The Clark County Health Department offered the free testing.

The "kick off" dinner was held on Saturday. We wanted to pay a guest speaker for the dinner, but again funds were limited. Working together, we used our own resources. The representative from the health department spoke about the statistics and prevention of AIDS (free service to educate the public). A woman in our group had lost her son to AIDS and offered to speak. "From a Mother's Heart" was the title of her speech. And I spoke about my experiences being married to a man living on the "down low," and how this phenomenon was one of the leading causes in the alarming rise of new HIV cases in our community. According to the latest statistics, African-American women are thirteen times more likely to contract HIV than their white counterparts. That crisis can be directly tied to men lying about their sexual preferences.

After the event, several women approached me to share their similar experiences and the pain they had to endure in secret for so long. They thanked me for being so honest.

We had expected a low attendance that day. But our first-ever Week of Prayer for AIDS turned out to be a huge success. It was standing room only. And our AIDS ministry is growing by the day. The mother who spoke at our event who lost her son to the disease is opening the Kenneth Hagan Center for AIDS in honor of her son. The group of nine churches plan to continue working together and assisting her with this project.

And I have expanded our ministry by offering counseling to women in my church. I have delivered several sermons on dealing with and overcoming adversity. But my greatest advice is for people to forgive. They need to forgive—forgive themselves first because too many beat themselves up, thinking that it is their fault when it's not. Then we need to forgive those who hurt us.

Forgiveness starts with knowing God and God's plan for your life. And knowing that He has greater things in store for you. As a young girl growing up in Springfield, Ohio, I only dreamed of being the perfect wife and mother. I had a typical life waiting for me. That's not what God had planned for me. He brought me through those trials and tribulations so I could learn more about me and so that I could be prepared for the real life He had for me.

I delivered the following sermon on May 30, 2003, before the Second Missionary Baptist Church in Springfield, Ohio:

God wants to use you. But God cannot use anyone who is bitter. You have to make a choice: bitter or better.

The only way to not be bitter is to study the truth in God's word, practice it, and then let God use you. One who is obedient to God and has a willing heart becomes a changed vessel. A willing heart means that you are willing to allow God to use you in situations that in your own mind you would rather avoid, and don't feel equipped to handle. God does not call the equipped, but equips those He calls. Be willing to forget about yourself and what you cannot do and obey Him.

When God called Moses, he did not feel equipped. So much so that Moses ran away from his calling for forty years. He didn't feel eloquent enough to talk to the pharaoh. He didn't feel strong enough to lead his people out of Egypt. And perhaps on his own he was not. In the beginning Moses didn't have enough faith to know that God would equip him with every tool he needed to complete the job. When Moses finally decided to obey, he not only overcame the things he felt he could not do, he was victorious in the mission God sent him on.

It will be no different for you or me.

Be a willing vessel to let the will of God prevail. God wants to use His people, people with transformed minds and hearts. The good thing is that we already have spiritual gifts just waiting to be developed to help build the Kingdom of God.

Romans, Chapter 12, Verses 6 to 8 (NIV), tells us that we have different gifts, according to the grace given us. If a man's gift is prophesying, let him use it in proportion to his faith. If it is serving, let him serve; if it is teaching, let him teach; if it is encouraging, let him encourage; if it is contributing to the needs of others, let him give generously; if it is leadership, let him govern diligently; if it is showing mercy, let him do it cheerfully.

But those gifts are like muscles; if not used, they will atrophy. If you don't exercise your spiritual gifts, they will wither away to nothing. And the only way to exercise them is to use them, put them into practice.

Sometimes we make choices in our young lives. We make these choices when we are young in physical body and young in the mind. Sometimes while young in our walk with God, we make choices that will alter or postpone the blessings that God wants to bring into our lives. Ultimately, our choices either make us bitter or they make us better

Friends, we don't have time to be bitter. God has given us this time that we have on earth to get better, so that we can serve Him and have a place in the Kingdom of God.

Ephesians, Chapter 4, Verses 31 to 32, says to put away from you all bitterness and wrath and anger and wrangling and slander, together with all malice, and be kind to one another, tenderhearted, forgiving one another, as God in Christ has forgiven you.

Oh be careful when you ask God to use you. God will not allow things to happen to make you weak, but strong. God will build some character in you if you let him; oh be careful when you ask to be of His service. Expect God to take you up on that. God will use that bitter situation. What do you have that God wants to use to help other people?

The first time that I was reluctant to share my secret in public, three women thanked me. They said they needed to hear that they were not by themselves, that they were not alone in their experience.

I asked God four years ago to use me. And He has. He took what I thought was a situation in my life that I would never overcome and turned it into an opportunity to help others. He used that situation, and He used me to make me better so that others can be healed.

Bitter or better?

In James, Chapter 3, Verses 14 to 18, it says: But if you have bitter envy and selfish ambition in your hearts, do not be boastful and false to the truth. Such wisdom does not come down from above, but is earthly, unspiritual, devilish. For where there is envy and selfish ambition, there will also be disorder and wickedness of every kind. But the wisdom from above is first pure, then peaceable, gentle, willing to yield, full of mercy and good fruits, without a trace of partiality or hypocrisy. And a harvest of righteousness sown in peace for those who make peace.

Bitter or better?

God gives us trials to build character. I can see there are some strong women here today. There are women who have been through many different trials. Maybe some

more than others. Death, depression, obsti-
nate children, sick parents, divorce, loss of
job, loneliness, more month than money,
drug abuse, aging, abusive relationships,
gossip, lying, abortion, menopause, rape.
I'm here to tell you that we serve an awesome God, a God bigger than our situations, a God with the power to deliver us
from all things. I'm here to tell you that you
are more than a conqueror.

Most times the problem lies in not what
the situation is but how we react to that situation. We can be mad, angry, resentful,
ashamed, arrogant, and deceitful, or we can
choose to get better in our situation. When
you choose to get better, you can soar like
an eagle, you can walk and not get weary,
you can run and not faint, you can mount
up with wings as an eagle, and fly!

Fly! Above your situation with the help
of the Holy Spirit, because God made you
fearfully and wonderfully to overcome your
situation. God is a loving God; God is a
forgiving God. Trust in the Lord to bring
you out of any adversity. You have power
when you serve the Lord to fly higher than
your situation but only when you let go of
your situation and let God handle it.

We all have been talked about, lied on,
cheated on; it doesn't matter, for if you let

God handle the situation, He will make your enemies your footstool.

Let's take a minute to look at this thing called a footstool. Today we look at a footstool as a place to rest our weary feet, to prop up on, to "take a load off." A footstool is a thing that is lower than your body. God's promise is real. Your enemies will be below you and will provide you with a place of rest.

Bitter or better?

When you release the bitter and focus on the positive and the good, you can enjoy the fruit of the spirit. You open the floodgates to love, joy, peace, patience, kindness, generosity, faithfulness, gentleness, and self-control to enter into your life.

Let go of that hurt, let go of that pain, show genuine forgiveness to your enemies. Let God control the situation. Everyone wants to be in control. But only God is in control, so you might as well let go and let God do His thing.

When I stop to think about the situations that I thought I was in control of, what a mess I made. I cried to God, "Fix this!" I could have remained bitter and never gotten it all fixed.

Bitterness promotes health problems. When

you are bitter or angry, your blood pressure rises, your sugar level goes up, that migraine begins to set in, your back starts to act up again. Let God handle the situation.

How do I let God handle the situation? Do nothing and let God work. You don't have to retaliate or get even with someone who has wronged you; pray for that person. You don't have to try to judge that person. Instead, look in the mirror and fix yourself. Watch your words and deeds and make sure you are correct and know God will fix them.

When an enemy strikes your face, the Bible tells us to turn the other cheek. When we finally let go of our bitterness and befriend our enemies, and let go of adversity, it allows God to bless us.

Patti LaBelle wrote a book called Don't Block the Blessings. *Being bitter blocks your blessings. Don't block your blessings with bitterness.*

My prayer for you all is that God keeps you from bitterness. That God will allow you to use your situation to help others. And that you will have the love of Christ for your brothers and sisters. I pray that the Holy Spirit reigns in your life and gives you the power to rise above your situation and that you will use it to serve and love others.

*I want to encourage you today and invite
you to read Psalm 51. It always reminds us
to never be bitter and always be better.*

Discussion Questions

1. Are you the type of woman that a DL man would prey on?
2. How do you approach your partner about testing for HIV and AIDS?
3. Can that request ruin the relationship?
4. Is homosexuality a sin to you?
5. Do you know someone who is in a relationship with someone on the DL or who is gay? And how did they deal with it?
6. Would you stay with your man if you found out he was gay?
7. Under what circumstances should you stay with a partner who has admitted that they were gay?
8. What were you taught about sexuality and where did you learn it?
9. What were your taught about homosexuality?
10. Was homosexuality ever discussed in your home and if so, how was it presented?
11. At what age should sexuality be discussed with your children?
12. What position should the church take on homosexuality, DL, same-sex marriages, etc?

Acknowledgments

Thank you, God. Thank you for a second chance. Thank you for Your grace. Thank you for Your mercy.

To my husband, Loren Franklin Browder Jr.: I love you. From Vietnam to now, you are strong. Yes, ladies, there are still strong black men!

To my children: Ebony and Brandon and Loren III, forever imprints in my heart. I am proud of you all. I know this has not been easy. I love you! I love you!

To my parents, Irvine and Parolee Stone (rest their souls): It wasn't easy raising seven children. Thank you. Mama, you graduated high school despite your obstacles, and Dad, you completed the eighth grade but somehow you instilled into your children—all college graduates—the importance of education. Most importantly, you instilled in us the importance of a relationship with God.

Thank you to my brothers and sisters: Dorothy, Irvine Jr., Janet, Kenneth, Gail, and John. You are all a part of me. As your baby sister, I really have been listening to all of the advice; thank you for paving the way. Daddy always said, "I love you all the same." Barbara, my angel, you went before us. Thank you, thank you.

Wilma, you mean so much to me. (Are you my sister-in-law?) Willie Mae, maybe some of your class has rubbed off on me. To Marshall and Glenda, you are prayer warriors. Thank you. Charles, thank you. This family has been quite interesting, huh? I love you all.

Roxanne, another angel, I miss you. Thank you for all of your prayers for me to have a relationship with God.

To my blended family: Kelli, Kim, and Celena, we have lived, laughed, cried, and prayed. Through it all, a black man still needs love. God's blessings. Tony, take care of your village. I am proud of you.

Shannon, my niece and my "running buddy," thank you for your love and support, and your work in HIV/AIDS prevention.

To Rita, my friend, in every sense of the word (you are still older than I am, but that makes you wiser).

To my cousin Angie Stone Clark, you still have the best sleepovers ever, Chicago Women's Retreat. "Cousin" Clarissa, we can still hang out, in church. Hallelujah!

Mary Daniel, thank you for your encouragement and prayers.

Pa King, I love you.

Pastor Dunbar, thank you for understanding how God is using me. To my family at Covenant, thank you for your prayers.

Benita, the prayers of the righteous availeth much; thank you for being obedient.

Thank you to the village: Aunt Beulah, Aunt Dorothy, Aunt Edna, Uncle Alfred, Uncle Mar, Aunt Evelyn, and Aunt Lydia.

To my nieces and nephews: You are a part of the village; be careful and love for keeps.

James Bush, you are wonderful. There is a woman missing out somewhere!

Mrs. Glenn and Mrs. Hagans, thanks to you for your brave innovative work in educating Springfield about HIV/AIDS. Juliet, Gina, Cheryl, Michael, Phil and Gail, your work in HIV/AIDS is necessary and effective, thank you.

Thank you, Karen Hunter, writer, for believing in me and for using your God-given talent to tell the story and make it happen—not only for me but for others, also. What do we say? "It's not about me."

Thank you, Karen Thomas, my editor, for wanting to know the wife's side of the story. To those at Kensington, you are great!

LaJoyce Brookshire, living your story was the test, telling your story was your testimony. You will enable other women to live in the promise of God for their lives, and their purpose in life. Thank you for being obedient to God, and for sharing your story.

Dr. Dansker, you told me, "When in doubt, leave it out." I took your advice.

Mrs. Lucas, when I think of an exemplary teacher, I think of you.

J.L., I can hear God saying, "My good and faithful servant." Through it all you have made a difference.

And to the readers of this book, God bless you. Be faithful!